The Way of Initiation
Or How to Attain Knowledge of the Higher Worlds

Rudolf Steiner

The Way of Initiation or, How to Attain Knowledge of the Higher Worlds

Copyright © 2022 Indo-European Publishing

All rights reserved

The present edition is a reproduction of previous publication of this classic work. Minor typographical errors may have been corrected without note; however, for an authentic reading experience the spelling, punctuation, and capitalization have been retained from the original text.

ISBN: 978-1-64439-689-6

CONTENTS

	The Personality of Rudolf Steinera His Development	1
I	The Superphysical World and Its Gnosis	22
II	How to Attain Knowledge of the Higher Worlds	36
III	The Path of Discipleship	47
IV	Probation	60
V	Enlightenment	69
VI	Initiation	88
VII	The Higher Education of the Soul	102
VIII	The Conditions of Discipleship	113

THE PERSONALITY OF RUDOLF STEINER AND HIS DEVELOPMENT

By Edouard Schuré[1]

Many of even the most cultivated men of our time have a very mistaken idea of what is a true mystic and a true occultist. They know these two forms of human mentality only by their imperfect or degenerate types, of which recent times have afforded but too many examples. To the intellectual man of the day, the mystic is a kind of fool and visionary who takes his fancies for facts; the occultist is a dreamer or a charlatan who abuses public credulity in order to boast of an imaginary science and of pretended powers. Be it remarked, to begin with, that this definition of mysticism, though deserved by some, would be as unjust as erroneous if one sought to apply it to such personalities as Joachim del Fiore of the thirteenth century, Jacob Boehme of the sixteenth, or St. Martin, who is called "the unknown philosopher," of the eighteenth century. No less unjust and false would be the current definition of the occultist if one saw in it the slightest connection with such earnest seekers as Paracelsus, Mesmer, or Fabre d'Olivet in the past, as William Crookes, de Rochat, or Camille Flammarion in the present. Think what we may of these bold investigators, it is undeniable that they have opened out regions unknown to science, and furnished the mind with new ideas.

---

[1] Translated by kind permission of the author from the introduction to Le Mystère Chrétien et les Mystères Antiques. Traduit de l'allemand par Edouard Schuré, Librairie académique, Perrin & Co., 1908, Paris.

No, these fanciful definitions can at most satisfy that scientific dilettantism which hides its feebleness under a supercilious mask to screen its indolence, or the worldly scepticism which ridicules all that threatens to upset its indifference. But enough of these superficial opinions. Let us study history, the sacred and profane books of all nations, and the last results of experimental science; let us subject all these facts to impartial criticism, inferring similar effects from identical causes, and we shall be forced to give quite another definition of the mystic and the occultist.

The true mystic is a man who enters into full possession of his inner life, and who, having become cognizant of his subconsciousness, finds in it, through concentrated meditation and steady discipline, new faculties and enlightenment. These new faculties and this enlightenment instruct him as to the innermost nature of his soul and his relations with that impalpable element which underlies all, with that eternal and supreme reality which religion calls God, and poetry the Divine. The occultist, akin to the mystic, but differing from him as a younger from an elder brother, is a man endowed with intuition and with synthesis, who seeks to penetrate the hidden depths and foundations of Nature by the methods of science and philosophy: that is to say, by observation and reason, methods invariable in principle, but modified in application by being adapted to the descending kingdoms of Spirit or the ascending kingdoms of Nature, according to the vast hierarchy of beings and the alchemy of the creative Word.

The mystic, then, is one who seeks for truth and the Divine directly within himself, by a gradual detachment and a veritable birth of his higher soul. If he attains it after prolonged effort, he plunges into his own glowing centre. Then he immerses himself, and identifies himself with that ocean of life which is the primordial Force.

The occultist, on the other hand, discovers, studies, and contemplates this same Divine outpouring given forth in diverse portions, endowed with force, and multiplied to infinity in Nature and in Humanity. According to the profound saying of Paracelsus: he sees in all beings the letters of an alphabet, which, united in man, form the complete and conscious Word of life. The detailed analysis that he makes of them, the syntheses that he constructs with them, are to him as so many images and forecastings of this central Divine, of this Sun of Beauty, of Truth and of Life, which he sees not, but which is reflected and bursts upon his vision in countless mirrors.

The weapons of the mystic are concentration and inner vision; the weapons of the occultist are intuition and synthesis. Each corresponds to the other; they complete and presuppose each other.

These two human types are blended in the Adept, in the higher Initiate. No doubt one or the other, and often both, are met with in the founders of great religions and the loftiest philosophies. No doubt also they are to be found again, in a less, but still very remarkable degree, among a certain number of personages who have played a great part in history as reformers, thinkers, poets, artists, statesmen.

Why, then, should these two types of mind, which represent the highest human faculties, and were formerly the object of universal veneration, usually appear to us now as merely deformed and travestied? Why have they become obliterated? Why should they have fallen into such discredit?

That is the result of a profound cause existing in an inevitable necessity of human evolution.

During the last two thousand years, but especially since the sixteenth century, humanity has achieved a tremendous work, namely, the conquest of the globe and the constitution of experimental science, in what concerns the material and visible world.

That this gigantic and herculean task should be successfully accomplished, it was necessary that there should be a temporary eclipse of man's transcendental faculties, so that his whole power of observation might be concentrated on the outer world. These faculties, however, have never been extinct or even inactive. They lay dormant in the mass of men; they remained active in the elect, far from the gaze of the vulgar.

Now, they are showing themselves openly under new forms. Before long they will assume a leading and directing importance in human destinies. I would add that at no period of history, whether among the nations of the ancient Aryan cycle, or in the Semitic civilizations of Asia and Africa—whether in the Græco-Latin world, or in the middle ages and in modern times, have these royal faculties, for which positivism would substitute its dreary nomenclature, ever ceased to operate at the beginning and in the background of all great human creations and of all fruitful work. For how can we imagine a thinker, a poet, an inventor, a hero, a master of science or of art, a genius of any kind, without a mighty ray of those two master-faculties which make the mystic and the occultist—the inner vision and the sovereign intuition.

Rudolf Steiner is both a mystic and an occultist. These two natures appear in him in perfect harmony. One could not say which of the two predominates over the other. In intermingling and blending, they have become one homogeneous force. Hence a special development in which outward events play but a secondary part.

Dr. Steiner was born in Upper Austria in 1861. His earliest years were passed in a little town situated on the Leytha, on the borders of Styria, the Carpathians, and Hungary. From childhood his character was serious and concentrated. This was followed by a youth inwardly illuminated by the most marvellous intuitions, a young manhood encountering terrible trials, and a ripe age crowned by a mission which he had dimly foreseen from his earliest years, but which was only gradually formulated in the struggle for truth and life. This youth, passed in a mountainous and secluded region, was happy in its way, thanks to the exceptional faculties that he discovered in himself. He was employed in a Catholic church as a choir boy. The poetry of the worship, the profundity of the symbolism, had a mysterious attraction for him; but, as he possessed the innate gift of seeing souls, one thing terrified him. This was the secret unbelief of the priests, entirely engrossed in the ritual and the material part of the service. There was another peculiarity: no one, either then or later, allowed himself to talk of any gross superstition in his presence, or to utter any blasphemy, as if those calm and penetrating eyes compelled the speaker to serious thought. In this child, almost always silent, there grew up a quiet and inflexible will, to master things through understanding. That was easier for him than for others, for he possessed from the first that self-mastery, so rare even in the adult, which gives the mastery over others. To this firm will was added a warm, deep and almost painful sympathy; a kind of pitiful tenderness to all beings and even to inanimate nature. It seemed to him that all souls had in them something divine. But in what a stony crust is hidden the shining gold! In what hard rock, in what dark gloom lay dormant the precious essence! Vaguely as yet did this idea stir within him—he was to develop it later—that the divine soul is present in all men, but in a latent state. It is a sleeping captive that has to be awakened from enchantment.

To the sight of this young thinker, human souls became transparent, with their troubles, their desires, their paroxysms of hatred or of love. And it was probably owing to the terrible things he saw, that he spoke so little. And yet, what delights, unknown to the world, sprang from this involuntary clairvoyance! Among the remarkable inner revelations of this youth, I will instance only one which was extremely characteristic.

The vast plains of Hungary, the wild Carpathian forests, the old churches of those mountains in which the monstrance glows brightly as a sun in the darkness of the sanctuary, were not there for nothing, but they were helpful to meditation and contemplation.

At fifteen years of age, Steiner became acquainted with a

herbalist at that time staying in his country. The remarkable thing about this man was that he knew not only the species, families, and life of plants in their minutest details, but also their secret virtues. One would have said that he had spent his life in conversing with the unconscious and fluid soul of herbs and flowers. He had the gift of seeing the vital principle of plants, their etheric body, and what Occultism calls the elementals of the vegetable world. He talked of it as of a quite ordinary and natural thing. The calm and coolly scientific tone of his conversation still further excited the curiosity and admiration of the youth. Later on, Steiner knew that this strange man was a messenger from the Master, whom as yet he knew not, but who was to be his real initiator, and who was already watching over him from afar.

What the curious, double-sighted botanist told him, young Steiner found to be in accordance with the logic of things. That confirmed an inner feeling of long standing, and which more and more forced itself on his mind as the fundamental Law, and as the basis of the Great All. That is to say: the two-fold current which constitutes the very movement of the world, and which might be called the flux and reflux of the universal life.

We are all witnesses and are conscious of the outward current of evolution, which urges onward all beings of heaven and of earth—stars, plants, animals and humanity—and causes them to move forward towards an infinite future, without our perceiving the initial force which impels them and makes them go on without pause or rest. But there is in the universe an inverse current, which interposes itself and perpetually breaks in on the other. It is that of involution, by which the principles, forces, entities and souls which come from the invisible world and the kingdom of the Eternal infiltrate and ceaselessly intermingle with the visible reality. No evolution of matter would be comprehensible without this occult and astral current, which is the great propeller of life, with its hierarchy of powers. Thus the Spirit, which contains the future in germ, involves itself in matter; thus matter, which receives the Spirit, evolves towards the future. While, then, we are moving on blindly towards the unknown future, this future is approaching us consciously, infusing itself in the current of the world and man who elaborate it. Such is the two-fold movement of time, the out-breathing and the in-breathing of the soul of the world, which comes from the Eternal and returns thither.

From the age of eighteen, young Steiner possessed the spontaneous consciousness of this two-fold current—a consciousness which is the condition of all spiritual vision. This vital axiom was forced upon him by a direct and involuntary seeing of things. Thenceforth he had the unmistakable sensation of occult powers which were working behind and through him for his guidance. He gave heed to this force and obeyed its admonitions, for he felt in profound accordance with it.

This kind of perception, however, formed a separate category in his intellectual life. This class of truths seemed to him something so profound, so mysterious, and so sacred, that he never imagined it possible to express it in words. He fed his soul thereon, as from a divine fountain, but to have scattered a drop of it beyond would have seemed to him a profanation.

Beside this inner and contemplative life, his rational and

philosophic mind was powerfully developing. From sixteen to seventeen years of age, Rudolf Steiner plunged deeply into the study of Kant, Fichte and Schelling. When he came to Vienna some years after, he became an ardent admirer of Hegel, whose transcendental idealism borders on Occultism; but speculative philosophy did not satisfy him. His positive mind demanded the solid basis of the sciences of observation. So he deeply studied mathematics, chemistry, mineralogy, botany and zoology. "These studies," he said "afford a surer basis for the construction of a spiritual system of the universe than history and literature. The latter, wanting in exact methods, would then throw no side-lights on the vast domain of German science." Inquiring into everything, enamored of high art, and an enthusiast for poetry, Steiner nevertheless did not neglect literary studies. As a guide therein he found an excellent professor in the person of Julius Schröer, a distinguished scholar of the school of the brothers Grimm, who strove to develop in his pupils the art of oratory and of composition. To this distinguished man the young student owed his great and refined literary culture. "In the desert of prevailing materialism," says Steiner, "his house was to me an oasis of idealism."

But this was not yet the Master whom he sought. Amidst these varied studies and deep meditations, he could as yet discern the building of the universe but in a fragmentary way; his inborn intuition prevented any doubt of the divine origin of things and of a spiritual Beyond. A distinctive mark of this extraordinary man was that he never knew any of those crises of doubt and despair which usually accompany the transition to a definite conviction in the life of mystics and of thinkers. Nevertheless, he felt that the central light which illumines and penetrates the whole was still lacking in him. He had reached young manhood, with its terrible problems. What was he going to do with his life? The sphinx of destiny was facing him. How should he solve its problem?

It was at the age of nineteen that the aspirant to the mysteries met with his guide—the Master—so long anticipated.

It is an undoubted fact, admitted by occult tradition and confirmed by experience, that those who seek the higher truth from an impersonal motive find a master to initiate them at the right moment: that is to say, when they are ripe for its reception. "Knock, and it shall be opened to you," said Jesus. That is true with regard to everything, but above all with regard to truth. Only, the desire must be ardent as a flame, in a soul pure as crystal.

The Master of Rudolf Steiner was one of those men of power who live, unknown to the world, under cover of some civil state, to carry out a mission unsuspected by any but their fellows in the Brotherhood of self-sacrificing Masters. They take no ostensible part in human events. To remain unknown is the condition of their power, but their action is only the more efficacious. For they inspire, prepare and direct those who will act in the sight of all. In the present instance the Master had no difficulty in completing the first and spontaneous initiation of his disciple. He had only, so to speak, to point out to him his own nature, to arm him with his needful weapons. Clearly did he show him the connection between the official and the secret sciences; between the religious and the spiritual forces which are now contending for the guidance of humanity; the antiquity of the occult tradition which holds the hidden threads of history, which mingles them, separates, and re-unites them in the course of ages.

Swiftly he made him clear the successive stages of inner discipline, in order to attain conscious and intelligent clairvoyance. In a few months the disciple learned from oral teaching the depth and incomparable splendor of the esoteric synthesis. Rudolf Steiner had already sketched for himself his intellectual mission: "To re-unite Science and Religion. To bring back God into Science, and Nature into Religion. Thus to re-fertilize both Art and Life." But how to set about this vast and daring undertaking? How conquer, or rather, how tame and transform the great enemy, the materialistic science of the day, which is like a terrible dragon covered with its carapace and couched on its huge treasure? How master this dragon of modern science and yoke it to the car of spiritual truth? And, above all, how conquer the bull of public opinion?

Rudolf Steiner's Master was not in the least like himself. He had not that extreme and feminine sensibility which, though not excluding energy, makes every contact an emotion and instantly turns the suffering of others into a personal pain. He was masculine in spirit, a born ruler of men, looking only at the species, and for whom individuals hardly existed. He spared not himself, and he did not spare others. His will was like a ball which, once shot from the cannon's mouth, goes straight to its mark, sweeping off everything in its way. To the anxious questioning of his disciple he replied in substance:

"If thou wouldst fight the enemy, begin by understanding him.

Thou wilt conquer the dragon only by penetrating his skin. As to the bull, thou must seize him by the horns. It is in the extremity of distress that thou wilt find thy weapons and thy brothers in the fight. I have shown thee who thou art, now go—and be thyself!"

Rudolf Steiner knew the language of the Masters well enough to understand the rough path that he was thus commanded to tread; but he also understood that this was the only way to attain the end. He obeyed, and set forth.

From 1880 the life of Rudolf Steiner becomes divided into three quite distinct periods: from twenty to thirty years of age (1881-1891), the Viennese period, a time of study and of preparation; from thirty to forty (1891-1901), the Weimar period, a time of struggle and combat; from forty to forty-six (1901-1907), the Berlin period, a time of action and of organization, in which his thought crystallized into a living work.

I pass rapidly over the Vienna period, in which Steiner took the degree of Doctor of Philosophy. He afterwards wrote a series of scientific articles on zoology, geology, and the theory of colors, in which theosophical ideas appear in an idealist clothing. While acting as tutor in several families, with the same conscientious devotion that he gave to everything, he conducted as chief editor a weekly Viennese paper, the Deutsche Wochenschrift. His friendship with the Austrian poetess, Marie Eugénie delle Grazie, cast, as it were, into this period of heavy work a warm ray of sunshine, with a smile of grace and poetry.

In 1890 Steiner was summoned to collaborate in the archives of Goethe and Schiller at Weimar, to superintend the re-editing of

Goethe's scientific works. Shortly after, he published two important works, Truth and Science and The Philosophy of Liberty. "The occult powers that guided me," he says, "forced me to introduce spiritualistic ideas imperceptibly into the current literature of the time." But in these various tasks he was but studying his ground while trying his strength. So distant was the goal that he did not dream of being able to reach it as yet. To travel round the world in a sailing vessel, to cross the Atlantic, the Pacific and the Indian Ocean, in order to return to a European port, would have seemed easier to him. While awaiting the events that would allow him to equip his ship and to launch it on the open sea, he came into touch with two illustrious personalities who helped to determine his intellectual position in the contemporary world.

These two persons were the celebrated philosopher, Friedrich Nietzsche, and the no less famous naturalist, Ernst Haeckel.

Rudolf Steiner had just written an impartial treatise on the author of Zarathustra. In consequence of this, Nietzsche's sister begged the sympathetic critic to come and see her at Naumburg, where her unhappy brother was slowly dying. Madame Foerster took the visitor to the door of the apartment where Nietzsche was lying on a couch in a comatose condition, inert, stupified. To Steiner there was something very significant in this melancholy sight. In it he saw the final act in the tragedy of the would-be superman.

Nietzsche, the author of Beyond Good and Evil, had not, like the realists of Bismarckian imperialism, renounced idealism, for he was naturally intuitive; but in his individualistic pride he sought to cut off the spiritual world from the universe, and the divine from human consciousness. Instead of placing the superman, of whom he had a poetic vision, in the spiritual kingdom, which is his true sphere, he strove to force him into the material world, which alone was real in his eyes. Hence, in that splendid intellect arose a chaos of ideas and a wild struggle which finally brought on softening of the brain. To explain this particular case, it is needless to bring in atavism or the theory of degeneracy. The frenzied combat of ideas and of contradictory sentiments, of which this brain was the battlefield, was enough. Steiner had done justice to all the genius that marked the innovating ideas of Nietzsche, but this victim of pride, self-destroyed by negation, was to him none the less a tragic instance of the ruin of a mighty intellect which madly destroys itself in breaking away from spiritual intelligence.

Madame Foerster did her utmost to enrol Dr. Steiner under her brother's flag. For this she used all her skill, making repeated offers to the young publicist to become editor and commentator of Nietzsche's works. Steiner withstood her insistence as best he could, and ended by taking himself off altogether, for which Madame Foerster never forgave him. She did not know that Rudolf Steiner bore within him the consciousness of a work no less great and more valuable than that of her brother.

Nietzsche had been merely an interesting episode in the life of the esoteric thinker on the threshold of his battlefield. His meeting with the celebrated naturalist, Ernst Haeckel, on the contrary, marks a most important phase in the development of his thought. Was not the successor of Darwin apparently the most formidable adversary of the spiritualism of this young initiate, of that philosophy which to him was the very essence of his being and the breath of his thought? Indeed, since the broken link between man and animal has been re-joined, since man can no longer believe in a special and supernatural origin, he has begun altogether to doubt his divine origin and destiny. He no longer sees himself as anything but one phenomenon among so many phenomena, a passing form amidst so many forms, a frail and chance link in a blind evolution. Steiner, then, is right in saying: "The mentality deduced from natural sciences is the greatest power of modern times." On the other hand, he knew that this system merely reproduces a succession of external forms among living beings, and not the inner and acting forces of life. He knew it from personal initiation, and a deeper and vaster view of the universe. So also he could exclaim with more assurance than most of our timid spiritualists and startled theologians: "Is the human soul then to rise on the wings of enthusiasm to the summits of the True, the Beautiful and the Good, only to be swept away into nothingness, like a bubble of the brain?" Yes, Haeckel was the Adversary. It was materialism in arms, the dragon with all his scales, his claws, and his teeth.

Steiner's desire to understand this man, and to do him justice as to all that was great in him, to fathom his theory so far as it was logical and plausible, was only the more intense. In this fact one sees all the loyalty and all the greatness of his comprehensive mind.

The materialistic conclusions of Haeckel could have no influence on his own ideas which came to him from a different science; but he had a presentment that in the indisputable discoveries of the naturalist he should find the surest basis of an evolutionary spiritualism and a rational theosophy.

He began, then, to study eagerly the History of Natural Creation. In it Haeckel gives a fascinating picture of the evolution of species, from the amœba to man. In it he shows the successive growth of organs, and the physiological process by which living beings have raised themselves to organisms more and more complex and more and more perfect. But in this stupendous transformation, which implies millions and millions of years, he never explains the initial force of this universal ascent, nor the series of special impulses which cause beings to rise step by step. To these primordial questions, Haeckel has never been able to reply except by admitting spontaneous generation,[2] which is tantamount to a miracle as great as the creation of man by God from a clod of earth. To a theosophist like Steiner, on the other hand, the cosmic force which elaborates the world comprises in its spheres, fitted one into another, the myriads of souls which crystallize and incarnate ceaselessly in all beings. He, who saw the underside of creation, could but recognize and admire the extent of the all-round gaze with which Haeckel surveyed his above. It was in vain that the naturalist would deny the divine Author of the universal scheme: he proved it in spite of himself, in so well describing His work. As to the theosophist, he greeted, in the surging of species and in the breath which urges them onward—Man in the making, the very thought of God, the visible expression of the planetary Word.[3]

---

[2] A speech delivered in Paris, 28th August 1878. See also Haeckel's History of Natural Creation, 13th lecture.
[3] This is how Dr. Steiner himself describes the famous German naturalist: "Haeckel's personality is captivating. It is the most complete contrast to the tone of his writings. If Haeckel had but made a slight study of the philosophy of which he speaks, not even as a dilettante,

While thus pursuing his studies, Rudolf Steiner recalled the saying of his Master: "To conquer the dragon, his skin must be penetrated." While stealing within the carapace of present-day materialism, he had seized his weapons. Henceforth he was ready for the combat. He needed but a field of action to give battle, and a powerful aid to uphold him therein. He was to find his field in the Theosophical Society, and his aid in a remarkable woman.

In 1897 Rudolf Steiner went to Berlin to conduct a literary magazine and to give lectures there.

On his arrival, he found there a branch of the Theosophical Society. The German branch of this Society was always noted for its great independence, which is natural in a country of transcendental philosophy and of fastidious criticism. It had already made a considerable contribution to occult literature through the interesting periodical, The Sphinx, conducted by Dr. Hübbe-Schleiden, and Dr. Carl du Prel's book—Philosophie der Mystik. But, the leaders having retired, it was almost over with the group. Great discussions and petty wranglings divided the theosophists beyond the Rhine. Should Rudolf Steiner enter the

---

but like a child, he would have drawn the most lofty spiritual conclusions from his phylogenetic studies. Haeckel's doctrine is grand, but Haeckel himself is the worst of commentators on his doctrine. It is not by showing our contemporaries the weak points in Haeckel's doctrine that we can promote intellectual progress, but by pointing out to them the grandeur of his phylogenetic thought." Steiner has developed these ideas in two works: Welt und Lebensanschauungen im 19ten Jahrhundert (Theories of the Universe and of Life in the Nineteenth Century), and Haeckel und seine Gegner (Haeckel and his Opponents).

Theosophical Society? This question forced itself urgently upon him, and it was of the utmost gravity, both for himself and for his cause.

Through his first Master, through the brotherhood with which he was associated, and by his own innermost nature, Steiner belongs to another school of Occultism, I mean to the esoteric Christianity of the West, and most especially to the Rosicrucian initiation.

After mature consideration he resolved to join the Theosophical Society of which he became a member in 1902. He did not, however, enter it as a pupil of the Eastern tradition, but as an initiate of Rosicrucian esotericism who gladly recognized the profound depth of the Hindu Wisdom and offered it a brotherly hand to make a magnetic link between the two. He understood that the two traditions were not meant to contend with each other, but to act in concert, with complete independence, and thus to work for the common good of civilization. The Hindu tradition, in fact, contains the greatest treasure of occult science as regards cosmogony and the prehistoric periods of humanity, while the tradition of Christian and Western esotericism looks from its immeasurable height upon the far-off future and the final destinies of our race. For the past contains and prepares the future, as the future issues from the past and completes it.

Rudolf Steiner was assisted in his work by a powerful recruit and one of inestimable value in the propagandist work that he was about to undertake.

Mlle. Marie von Sivers, a Russian by birth, and of an unusually varied cosmopolitan education (she writes and speaks Russian,

French, German, and English equally well), had herself also reached Theosophy by other roads, after long seeking for the truth which illumines all because it illumines the very depths of our own being. The extreme refinement of her aristocratic nature, at once modest and proud, her great and delicate sensitiveness, the extent and balance of her intelligence, her artistic and mental endowments, all made her wonderfully fitted for the part of an agent and an apostle. The Oriental theosophy had attracted and delighted her without altogether convincing her. The lectures of Dr. Steiner gave her the light which convinces by casting its beams on all sides, as from a transplendent centre. Independent and free, she, like many Russians in good society, sought for some ideal work to which she could devote all her energies. She had found it. Dr. Steiner having been appointed General Secretary of the German Section of the Theosophical Society, Mlle. Marie von Sivers became his assistant. From that time, in spreading the work throughout Germany and the adjacent countries, she displayed a real genius for organization, maintained with unwearied activity.

As for Rudolf Steiner, he had already given ample proof of his profound thought and his eloquence. He knew himself, and he was master of himself. But such faith, such devotion must have increased his energy a hundredfold, and given wings to his words. His writings on esoteric questions followed one another in rapid succession.[4]

---

[4] Die Mystik, im Aufgange des neuzeitlichen Geisteslebens (1901); Das Christentum als mystische Tatsache (1902); Theosophie (1904). He is now preparing an important book, which will no doubt be his chief work, and which is to be called Geheimwissenschaft (Occult Science).

He delivered lectures in Berlin, Leipzig, Cassel, Munich, Stuttgart, Vienna, Budapest, etc. All his books are of a high standard. He is equally skilled in the deduction of ideas in philosophical order, and in rigorous analysis of scientific facts. And when he so chooses, he can give a poetical form to his thought, in original and striking imagery. But his whole self is shown only by his presence and his speech, private or public. The characteristic of his eloquence is a singular force, always gentle in expression, resulting undoubtedly from perfect serenity of soul combined with wonderful clearness of mind. Added to this at times is an inner and mysterious vibration which makes itself felt by the listener from the very first words. Never a word that could shock or jar. From argument to argument, from analogy to analogy, he leads you on from the known to the unknown. Whether following up the comparative development of the earth and of man, according to occult tradition, through the Lemurian, Atlantean, Asiatic and European periods; whether explaining the physiological and psychic constitution of man as he now is; whether enumerating the stages of Rosicrucian initiation, or commenting on the Gospel of St. John and the Apocalypse, or applying his root-ideas to mythology, history and literature, that which dominates and guides his discourse is ever this power of synthesis, which co-ordinates facts under one ruling idea and gathers them together in one harmonious vision. And it is ever this inward and contagious fervor, this secret music of the soul, which is, as it were, a subtle melody in harmony with the Universal Soul.

Such, at least, is what I felt on first meeting him and listening to him two years ago. I could not better describe this undefinable feeling than by recalling the saying of a poet-friend to whom I was showing the portrait of the German theosophist. Standing before those deep and clear-seeing eyes, before that countenance, hollowed by inward struggles, moulded by a lofty spirit which has proved its balance on the heights and its calm in the depths, my friend exclaimed: "Behold a master of himself and of life!"

THE WAY OF INITIATION

I

THE SUPERPHYSICAL WORLD AND ITS GNOSIS

In this practical age and because of the many various claims of the day, it is but natural that people, who hear of transcendentalism should at once ask the question: "How may we for ourselves know the truth of such statements?" Indeed, it is noticeable, as a characteristic of the majority, that they will accept nothing on faith, or mere "authority," but wish rather to rely entirely upon their own judgment. Therefore, when a mystic undertakes to explain something of the superphysical nature of man, and of the destiny of the human soul and spirit before birth and after death, he is at once confronted with that fundamental demand. Such doctrine, they seem to think is important only when you have shown them the way by which they may convince themselves of its truth.

This critical inquiry is quite justified; and no true mystic or occultist will dispute its fairness, yet it is unfortunate that with many who make the demand, there exists a feeling of skepticism or antagonism toward the mystic or any attempt on his part to explain anything occult. This feeling becomes especially marked when the mystic intimates how the truths which he has described may be attained. For they say, "Whatever is true may be demonstrated; therefore, prove to us what you assert." They demand that the truth must be something clear and simple, something which an ordinary intellect may comprehend. "Surely," they add, "this knowledge cannot be the possession of a chosen few, to whom it is given by a special revelation." And in this way the real messenger of transcendental truth is frequently confronted with people who reject him, because—unlike the scientist, for example, he can produce no proofs for his assertions, of such a nature as they are able to understand. Again, there are those who cautiously reject any information pertaining to the superphysical because to them it does not seem reasonable. Thereupon they partially satisfy themselves, by claiming that we cannot know anything of what lies beyond birth or death, or of anything which cannot be perceived through our five ordinary physical senses.

These are but a few of the arguments and criticisms with which to-day the messenger of a spiritual philosophy is confronted; but they are similar to all those which compose the key-note of our time, and he who puts himself at the service of a spiritual movement must recognize this condition quite clearly.

For his own part, the mystic is aware that his knowledge rests upon superphysical facts; which to him are just as tangible, for example, as those that form the foundation of the experiences and observations described by a traveller in Africa or any strange land. To the mystic applies what Annie Besant has said in her manual, "Death and After?"

> "A seasoned African explorer would care but little for the criticisms passed on his report by persons who had never been there; he might tell what he saw, describe

> the animals whose habits he had studied, sketch the country he had traversed, sum up its products and its characteristics. If he was contradicted, laughed at, set right, by untravelled critics, he would be neither ruffled nor distressed, but would merely leave them alone. Ignorance cannot convince knowledge by repeated asseveration of its nescience. The opinion of a hundred persons on a subject of which they are wholly ignorant is of no more weight than the opinion of one such person. Evidence is strengthened by many consenting witnesses, testifying each to his knowledge of a fact, but nothing multiplied a thousand times remains nothing."

Here is expressed the mystic's view of his own situation. He hears the objections which are raised on every side, yet he knows that for himself he has no need to dispute them. He realizes that his certain knowledge is being criticized by those who have not had his experience, that he is in the position of a mathematician who has discovered a truth which can lose no value though a thousand voices are raised in opposition.

Then again will arise the objection of the skeptics: "Mathematical truths may be proven to anyone," they will say, "and though perhaps you have really found something, we shall accept it only when we have learned of its truth through our own investigation." Such then have reason to consider themselves to be in the right, because it is clear to them that anyone who acquires the necessary knowledge can prove a mathematical truth, while the experiences professed by the mystic if true depend upon the special faculties of a few elect mystics, in whom they assume they are expected to blindly believe.

For him, who rightly considers this objection, all justification for the doubt immediately vanishes; and mystics can here use the very logical reasoning of the skeptics themselves, by emphasizing the truth that the way to Higher Knowledge is open to anyone who will acquire for himself the faculties by which he may prove the spiritual truths herein claimed. The mystic asserts nothing which his opponents would not also be compelled to assert, if they did but fully comprehend their own statements. They, however, in making an assertion, often formulate a claim which constitutes a direct contradiction of that assertion.

Skeptics are seldom willing to acquire the necessary faculties to test the assertions of the mystic, but prefer to judge him offhand, without regard to their own lack of qualification. The sincere mystic says to them: "I do not claim to be 'chosen' in the sense that you mean. I have merely developed within myself, some of man's additional senses in order to acquire the faculties through which it is possible to speak of glimpses into superphysical regions." These senses are dormant within you and every other person, until they are developed, (as is necessary with the usual senses and faculties more noticeable in the growth of a child). Yet his opponents answer: "You must prove your truths to us as we now are!" This at once appears a difficult task, for they have not complied with the necessity of developing the dormant powers within them, they are still unwilling to do so, and yet they insist that he shall give them proofs; nor do they see that this is exactly as if a peasant at his plough should demand of the mathematician the proof of a complicated problem, without his undergoing the trouble of learning mathematics.

This mixed mental condition appears to be so general and its solution so simple that one almost hesitates to speak of it. And yet it indicates a delusion under which millions of people continue living at the present time. When explained to them they always agree in theory, since it is quite as plain as, that two and two make four; yet in practice they continually act in contradiction. The mistake has grown to be second nature with many; they indulge it without realizing that they do so without desiring to be convinced of its error; just as they set themselves against other laws which they should and would at all times recognize as embodying a principle of the simplest nature, if they but gave it an unbiased consideration. It matters not whether the mystic of to-day moves among thinking artisans, or in a more educated circle, wherever he goes he meets with the same prejudice, the same self-contradiction. One finds it in popular lectures, in the newspapers and magazines, and even in the more learned works or treatises.

Here we must recognize quite clearly that we are dealing with a consensus of opinion that amounts to a sign of the times, which we may not simply pronounce as incompetent, nor deal with as possibly a correct but unjust criticism. We must understand that this prejudice against the higher truths, lies deep in the very being of our age. We must understand clearly that the great successes, the immense advance marking our time, necessarily encourages this condition. The nineteenth century especially had in the above respect a dark side to its wonderful excellences. Its greatness rests upon discoveries in the external world, and conquest of natural forces for technical and industrial purposes. These successes could have been attained only by the employment of the mind directed toward material results.

The civilization of the present day is the result of the training of our senses, and of that part of our mind which is occupied with the world of sense. Almost every step we take in the busy marts of to-day shows us how much we owe to this kind of training. And it is under the influence of these blessings of civilization that the habits of thought, prevalent among our fellow-men, have been developed. They continue to abide by the senses and the mind, because it is by means of these that they have grown great. People were taught to train themselves to admit nothing as true except those things that were presented to them by the senses or the intellect. And nothing is more apt to claim for itself the only valid testimony, the only absolute authority, than the mind or the senses. If a man has acquired by means of them a certain degree of culture, he thenceforth accustoms himself to submit everything to their consideration, everything to their criticism. And again in another sphere, in the domain of Social Life, we find a similar trait. The man of the nineteenth century insisted, in the fullest sense of the word, upon the absolute freedom of personality, and repudiated any authority in the Social Commonwealth. He endeavored to construct the community in such a way that the full independence, the self-chosen vocation of each individual, should, without interference, be assured. In this way it became habitual for him to consider everything from the standpoint of the average individual.

This same individuality is also helpful in the search of knowledge on the spiritual plane, for the higher powers which lie dormant in the soul may be developed by one person in this direction by another in that. One will make more progress, another less. But when they develop those powers, and attach value to them, men begin to differentiate themselves. And then one must allow, to the advanced student, more right to speak on the subject, or to act in a certain way, than to another who is less advanced. This is more essential in matters of the higher realm than on the plane of the senses and the mind, where experiences are more nearly the same.

It is also noticeable that the present formation of the Social Commonwealth has helped to bring about a revolt against the higher powers of man. According to the mystic, civilization during the nineteenth century has moved altogether along physical lines; and people have accustomed themselves to move on the physical plane alone, and to feel at home there. The higher powers are developed only on planes higher than the physical, and the knowledge which these faculties bring is, therefore, unknown to the physical man. It is only necessary to attend mass-meetings, if one wishes to be convinced of the fact that the speakers there are totally unable to think any thoughts but those which refer to the physical plane, the world of sense. This can also be seen through the leading journalists of our papers and magazines; and, indeed, on all sides one may observe the haughtiest and most complete denial of everything that cannot be seen with the eyes, or felt with the hands, or comprehended by the average mind. We do not condemn this attitude for it denotes a necessary stage in the development of humanity. Without the pride and prejudices of mind and sense, we should never have achieved our great conquests over material life, nor have been able to impart to the personality a certain measure of elasticity: neither can we hope that many ideals, which must be founded on man's desire for freedom and the assertion of personality, may yet be realized.

But this dark side of a purely materialistic civilization has deeply affected the whole being of the modern man. For proof it is not necessary to refer to the obvious facts already named; it would be easy to demonstrate, by certain examples (which are greatly underrated, especially to-day), how deeply rooted in the mind of the modern man is this adhesion to the testimony of the senses, or the average intelligence. And it is just these things that indicate the need for the renewal of spiritual life.

The strong response evoked by Professor Friedrich Delitzsch's Babel and Bible Theory fully justifies a reference to its author's method of thinking, as a sign of the time. Professor Delitzsch has demonstrated the relationship of certain traditions in the Old Testament, to the Babylonian accounts of the Creation, and this fact, coming from such a source and in such a form, has been realized by many who would otherwise have ignored such questions. It has led many to reconsider the so-called idea of Revelation. They ask themselves: "How is it possible to accept the idea that the contents of the Old Testament were revealed by God, when we find very similar conceptions among decidedly heathen nations?" This problem cannot here be further discussed. Delitzsch found many opponents who feared that through his exposition, the very foundations of Religion had been shaken. He has defended himself in a pamphlet, Babel and Bible, a Retrospect and a Forecast. Here we shall only refer to a single statement in the pamphlet. One of importance, because it reveals the view of an eminent scientist regarding the position of man with respect to transcendental truths. And to-day innumerable other people think and feel just like Delitzsch. The statement affords an excellent opportunity for us to find out what is the innermost conviction of our contemporaries, expressed quite freely and, therefore, in its truest form.

Delitzsch turns to those who reproach him with a somewhat liberal use of the term "Revelation," and who would fain regard it as "a kind of old priestly wisdom" which "has nothing at all to do with the layman," making this reply.

> "For my part, I am of opinion that while our children or ourselves are instructed in school or at church as regards Revelation, not only are we within our right, but it is our duty, to think independently concerning these deep questions, possessing also, as they do, an eminently practical side, were it only that we might avoid giving our children 'evasive' answers. For this very reason it will be gratifying to many searchers after Truth when the dogma of a special 'choosing' of Israel shall have been brought forward into the light of a wider historical outlook, through the union of Babylonian, Assyrian, and Old Testament research....
> [A few pages earlier we are shown the direction of such thoughts.] For the rest, it would seem to me that the only logical thing is for Church and School to be satisfied as regards the whole past history of the world and of humanity, with the belief in One Almighty Creator of Heaven and Earth, and that these tales of the Old Testament should be classified by themselves under some such title as 'Old Hebraic Myths.'"

(It may be taken as a matter of course, we suppose, that no one will see in the following remarks an attack on the investigator

Delitzsch.) What, then, is here averred in naive simplicity? Nothing less than that the mind which is engaged upon physical investigation may assert the right of judging experiences of superphysical nature. There is no thought that this mind without further development may perhaps be unfit to reflect upon the teachings of these "Revelations." When one wishes to understand that which appears as a "Revelation," one must employ the kind of knowledge or forces through which the "Revelation," itself has come to us.

He who develops within himself the mystical power of perception soon observes that in certain stories of the Old Testament which by Delitzsch were called "Old Hebraic Myths," there are revealed to him truths of a higher nature than those which may be comprehended by the intellect, which is only concerned with the things of sense. His own experiences will lead him to see that these "Myths" have proceeded out of a mystic perception of transcendental truths. And then, in one illuminative moment, his whole point of view is changed.

As little as one may demonstrate the fallacy of a mathematical problem by discovering who solved it first, or even that several people have solved it, just so little may one impugn the truth of a biblical narrative by the discovery of a similar story elsewhere. Instead of demanding that everyone should insist upon his right, or even his duty, to think independently on the so-called "Revelations," we ought rather to consider that only he who has developed in himself those latent powers which make it possible for him to relive that which was once realized by those very mystics, who proclaimed the "supersensuous revelations," has a right to decide anything about the matter.

Here we have an excellent example of how the average intellect, qualified for the highest triumphs in practical sense-knowledge, sets itself up, in naive pride, as a judge in domains, the existence of which it does not even care to know. For purely historical investigation is also carried on by nothing but the experience of the senses.

In just the same way has the investigation of the New Testament led us into a blind alley. At any costs the method of the "Newer Historical Investigation" had to be directed upon the Gospels. These documents have been compared with each other, and brought into relation with all sorts of records, in order that we might find out what really happened in Palestine from the year 1 to the year 33; how the "historical personality" of whom they tell really lived, and what He may really have said.

Angelus Selesius, of the seventeenth century, has already expressed the whole of the critical attitude toward this kind of investigation:

> "Though Christ were yearly born in Bethlehem, and never Had birth in you yourself, then were you lost for ever; And if within yourself it is not reared again, The Cross at Golgotha can save you not from pain."

Nor are these the words of one who doubted, but those of a Christian, strong in his belief. And his equally fervent predecessor, Meister Eckhart, said in the thirteenth century:

> "There are some who desire to see God with their eyes, as they look at a cow; and just as they love a cow, so they desire to love God.... Simple-minded people

imagine that God may be seen as if He stood there and they stood here. But this is not so: in that perception, God and I are one."

These words must not be understood as directed against the investigation of "historical truth." Yet no one can rightly understand the historic truth of such documents as the Gospels, unless he has first experienced within himself the mystical meaning which they contain. All such comparisons and analyses are quite worthless, for no one can discover who was "born in Bethlehem" but he who has mystically experienced the Christ within himself; neither can anyone in whom it has not already been erected, decide how it is that "the Cross at Golgotha" can deliver us from pain. Purely historical investigation "can discover no more concerning the mystic reality than the dismembering anatomist, perhaps, can discover the secret of a great poetical genius." (See my book, Das Christentum als mystische Tatsache, Berlin, C. A. Schwetschke und Sohn, 1902, or its French translation, mentioned on page 1.)

He who can see clearly in these matters is aware how deeply rooted, at the present time, is the "pride" of the intellect, which only concerns itself with the facts of sense. It says: "I do not wish to develop faculties in order that I may reach the higher truths; I wish to form my decisions concerning them with the powers that I now possess."

In a well-meant pamphlet, which is written, however, entirely in that spirit of the age which we have already indicated (What do we know about Jesus? by A. Kalthoff, Berlin, 1904), we read as follows:

"Christ, who symbolizes the life of the Community, may be discerned within himself by the man of to-day: out of his own soul the man of to-day can create Christ just as well as the author of a gospel created him; as a man he may put himself in the same position as the gospel-writers, because he can reinstate himself into the same soul-processes, can himself speak or write Gospel."

"These words might be true, but they may also be entirely erroneous. They are true when understood in the sense of Angelus Silesius, or of Meister Eckhart, that is when they refer to the development of powers dormant in every human soul, which, from some such idea, endeavors to experience within itself the Christ of the Gospels. They are altogether wrong, if a more or less shallow ideal of the Christ is thus created out of the spirit of an age that acknowledges the truth of no perceptions other than those of the senses."

The life of the Spirit can be understood only when we do not presume to criticize it with the lower mind, but rather when we develop it reverently within ourselves. No one can hope to learn anything of the higher truths if he demands that they shall be lowered to the "average understanding." This statement provokes the question: "Why, then, do you mystics proclaim these truths to people who, you declare, cannot as yet understand them? Why should there be Movements in the furtherance of certain teachings, when the powers which render men able to conceive of these teachings are still undeveloped?"

It is the task of this book to elucidate this apparent contradiction. It will show that the spiritual currents of our day originate from a different source, in a different manner, from the science which relies entirely on the lower intellect. Yet, in spite of this, these spiritual currents are not to be considered as less scientific than the science which is based upon physical facts alone. Rather do they extend the field of scientific investigation into the superphysical. We must close this chapter with one more question, which is likely to arise: How may one attain to superphysical truths, and, of what help are spiritual movements towards this attainment?

II

HOW TO ATTAIN KNOWLEDGE OF THE HIGHER WORLDS

In every man there are latent faculties by means of which he may acquire for himself knowledge of the higher worlds. The mystic, master, theosophist, or gnostic speaks of a soul-world and a spirit-world, which are, for him, just as real as the world which we see with our physical eyes, or touch with our physical hands. And those who wish to develop the spiritual senses, which unfold psychic knowledge, should understand that safe advice can be given only by those who have already developed such power within themselves. As long as the human race has existed, there have been lodges and schools in which those who possessed these higher faculties have given instruction to those who were in search of them. Such are called occult schools, and the instruction which is imparted therein is called esoteric science, or occult teaching. This designation sometimes leads to misunderstanding. He who hears it may be very easily misled into the belief that those who work in these schools desire to represent a special, privileged class, which arbitrarily withholds its knowledge from its fellow-creatures. Indeed, he may even think that perhaps there is nothing really important behind such knowledge. For he is tempted to think that, if it were a true knowledge, there would be no need of making a secret of it: one might then communicate it publicly to the advantage of all men.

Those who have been initiated into occult knowledge are not in the least surprised that the uninitiated should so think. Only he who has to a certain degree experienced this initiation into the higher knowledge of being can understand the secret of that initiation. But it may be asked: How, then, shall the uninitiated, considering the circumstances, develop any interest at all in this so-called mystic knowledge? How and why ought they to search for something of the nature of which they can form no idea? Such a question is based upon an entirely erroneous conception of the real nature of occult knowledge. There is, in truth, no fundamental difference between occult knowledge and all the rest of man's knowledge and capacity. This mystic knowledge is no more a secret for the average man than writing is a secret to him who has never learned to read. And just as everyone who chooses the correct method may learn to write, so too can everyone who searches after the right way become a disciple, and even a teacher. In only one respect are the conditions here different from those that apply to external thought-activities. The possibility of acquiring the art of writing may be withheld from someone through poverty, or through the state of civilization into which he has been born; but for the attainment of knowledge in the higher worlds there is no obstacle for him who sincerely searches for it.

Many believe that it is necessary to find, here or there, the Masters of the higher knowledge, in order to receive enlightenment from them. In the first place, he who strives earnestly after the higher knowledge need not be afraid of any difficulty or obstacle in his search for an Initiate who shall be able to lead him into the profounder secrets of the world. Everyone, on the contrary, may be certain that an Initiate will find him, under any circumstances, if there is in him an earnest and worthy endeavor to attain this knowledge. For it is a strict law with all Initiates to withhold from no man the knowledge that is due him. But there is an equally strict law which insists that no one shall receive any occult knowledge until he is worthy and well prepared. And the more strictly he observes these two laws, the more perfect is an Initiate. The order which embraces all Initiates is surrounded, as it were, by a wall, and the two laws here mentioned form two strong principles by which the constituents of this wall are held together. You may live in close friendship with an Initiate, yet this wall will separate him from you just as long as you have not become an Initiate yourself. You may enjoy in the fullest sense the heart, the love of an Initiate, yet he will only impart to you his secret when you yourself are ready for it. You may flatter him; you may torture him; nothing will induce him to divulge to you anything which he knows ought not be disclosed, inasmuch as you, at the present stage of your evolution, do not understand rightly how to receive the secret into your soul.

The ways which prepare a man for the reception of such a secret are clearly prescribed. They are indicated by the unfading, everlasting letters within the temples where the Initiates guard the higher secrets. In ancient times, anterior to "history," these temples were outwardly visible; to-day, because our lives have become so unspiritual, they are mostly quite invisible to external sight. Yet they are present everywhere, and all who seek may find them.

Only within his soul may a man discover the means which will open for him the lips of the Initiate. To a certain high degree he must develop within himself special faculties, and then the greatest treasures of the Spirit become his own.

He must begin with a certain fundamental attitude of the soul: the student of Occultism calls it the Path of Devotion, of Veneration. Only he who maintains this attitude can, in Occultism, become a disciple. And he who has experience in these things is able to perceive even in the child the signs of approaching discipleship. There are children who look up with religious awe to those whom they venerate. For such people they have a respect which forbids them to admit, even in the innermost sanctuary of the heart, any thought of criticism or opposition. These children grow up into young men and maidens who feel happy when they are able to look up to anything venerable. From the ranks of such children are recruited many disciples.

Have you ever paused outside the door of some venerated man, and have you, on this your first visit, felt a religious awe as you pressed the handle, in order to enter the room which for you is a holy place? Then there has been manifested in you an emotion which may be the germ of your future discipleship. It is a blessing for every developing person to have such emotions upon which to build. Only it must not be thought that such qualities contain the germ of submissiveness and slavery. Experience teaches us that those can best hold their heads erect who have learned to venerate where veneration is due. And veneration is always in its own place when it rises from the depths of the heart.

If we do not develop within ourselves this deeply-rooted feeling that there is something higher than ourselves, we shall never find enough strength to evolve to something higher. The Initiate has only acquired the power of lifting his intellect to the heights of knowledge by guiding his heart into the depths of veneration and devotion. The heights of the Spirit can only be reached by passing through the portals of humility. Man can certainly have the right to gaze upon the Reality, but he must first earn this right. You can only acquire right knowledge when you are ready to esteem it. There are laws in the spiritual life, as in the physical life. Rub a glass rod with an appropriate material and it will become electric, that is to say, it will acquire the power of attracting small bodies. This exemplifies natural law. (And if one has learned even a little of physics, one knows this.) Similarly, if one is acquainted with the first principles of Occultism, one knows that every feeling of true devotion aids in developing qualities, which sooner or later, lead to the Path of Knowledge.

He who possesses within himself this feeling of devotion, or who is fortunate enough to receive it from his education, brings a great deal along with him, when, later in life, he seeks an entrance to the higher knowledge. But he who has had no such preparation will find himself confronted with difficulties, even upon the first step of the Path of Knowledge, unless he undertakes, by rigorous self-education, to create the devotional mood within himself. In our time it is especially important that full attention be given to this point. Our civilization tends much more toward criticism, the giving of judgments, and so forth, than toward devotion, and a selfless veneration. Our children criticize much more than they worship. But every judgment, every carping criticism, frustrates the powers of the soul for the attainment of the higher knowledge, in the same measure that all heartfelt devotion develops them. In this we do not wish to say anything against our civilization nor pass judgment upon it. For it is to this critical faculty, this self-conscious human discernment, this "prove all things and hold fast to the good," that we owe the greatness of our civilization. We could never have attained the science, the commerce, the industry, the law of our time, had we not exercised our critical faculty everywhere, had we not everywhere applied the standard of our judgment. But what we have thereby gained in external culture we have had to pay for with a corresponding loss of the higher knowledge, of the spiritual life.

Now the important thing that everyone must clearly understand is that, for him who is right in the midst of the objective civilization of our time, it is very difficult to advance to the knowledge of the higher worlds. He can do so only if he work energetically within himself. At a time when the conditions of outward life were simpler, spiritual exaltation was easier of attainment. That which ought to be venerated, that which should be kept holy, stood out in better relief from the ordinary things of the world. In a period of criticism these ideals are much lowered; other emotions take the place of awe, veneration, respect, and prayer. Our own age continually pushes these better emotions further and further back, so that in the daily life of the people they play but a very small part. He who seeks for higher knowledge must create it within himself; he himself must instil it into his soul. It cannot be done by study; it can only be done through living. He who wishes to become a disciple must therefore assiduously cultivate the devotional mood.

Everywhere in his environment he must look for that which demands of him admiration and homage. Whenever his duties or circumstances permit, he should try to abstain entirely from all criticism or judgment. If I meet a brother and blame him for his weakness, I rob myself of power to win the higher knowledge; but if I try to enter lovingly into his merits, I then gather such power. The disciple should seek to benefit both himself and others. Experienced occultists are aware how much they owe to the continual searching for the good in all things, and the withholding of all harsh criticism. This must be not only an external rule of life; but it must take possession of the innermost part of our souls. We have it in our power to perfect ourselves, and by and by to transform ourselves completely. But this transformation must take place in the innermost self, in the mental life. It is not enough that I show respect only in my outward bearing toward a person; I must have this respect in my thought. The disciple must begin by drawing this devotion into his thought-life. He must altogether banish from his consciousness all thoughts of disrespect, of criticism, and he must endeavor straightway to cultivate thoughts of devotion.

Every moment, in which we set ourselves to banish from our consciousness whatever remains in it of disparaging, suspicious judgment of our fellow-men, brings us nearer to the knowledge of higher things. And we rise rapidly when, in such moments, we fill our consciousness with only those thoughts that evoke admiration, respect, and veneration for men and things. He who has experience in these matters will know that in every such moment powers are awakened in man which otherwise would remain dormant. In this way the spiritual eyes of a man are opened. He begins to see things around him which hitherto he was unable to perceive. He begins to understand that hitherto he had seen only a part of the world around him. The man with whom he comes in contact now shows him quite a different aspect from that which he showed before. Of course, through this single rule of life, he will not yet be able to see what has elsewhere been described as the human aura, because, for that, a still higher training is necessary. But he may rise to that higher development if he has previously had a thorough training in devotion.[5]

Noiseless and unnoticed by the outer world is the following of the "Path of Discipleship." It is not necessary that anyone should observe a change in the disciple. He performs his duties as hitherto; he attends to his business as usual. The transformation goes on only in the inner part of the soul, hidden from outward sight. At first the entire soul-life of a man is flooded by this fundamental spring of devotion for everything which is truly venerable. His entire soul-life finds in this devotional mood its pivot. Just as the sun, through its rays, will vivify everything living, so in the life of the disciple this reverence vivifies all the perceptions of the soul.

At first it is not easy for people to believe that feelings like reverence, respect, and so forth, have anything to do with their perceptions. This comes from the fact that one is inclined to think of perception as a faculty quite by itself, one that stands in no relation to what otherwise happens in the soul. In so

---

[5] In the last chapter of the book entitled Theosophie (Berlin, C. A. Schwetschke und Sohn), Dr. Rudolf Steiner fully describes this "Path of Knowledge;" here it is only intended to give some practical details.

thinking, we do not remember that it is the soul which perceives. And feelings are for the soul what food is for the body. If we give the body stones in place of bread its activity will cease. It is the same with the soul. Veneration, homage, devotion, are as nutriment which makes it healthy and strong, especially strong for the activity of perception. Disrespect, antipathy, and underestimation, bring about the starvation and the withering of this activity. For the occultist this fact is visible in the aura. A soul which harbors the feelings of devotion and reverence, brings about a change in its aura. Certain yellowish-red or brown-red tints will vanish, and tints of bluish-red will replace them. And then the organ of perception opens. It receives information of facts in its environment of which it hitherto had no knowledge. Reverence awakens a sympathetic power in the soul, and through this we attract similar qualities in the beings which surround us, that would otherwise remain hidden. More effective still is that power which can be obtained by devotion when another feeling is added. One learns to give up oneself less and less to the impressions of the outer world, and to develop in its place a vivid inward life. He who darts from one impression of the outer world to another, who constantly seeks dissipations, cannot find the way to Occultism. Neither should the disciple blunt himself to the outer world; but let his rich inner life point out the direction in which he ought to lend himself to its impressions. When passing through a beautiful mountain district, the man with depth of soul and richness of emotion has different experiences from the man with few emotions. Only what we experience within ourselves reveals the beauties of the outer world. One man sails across the ocean, and only a few inward experiences pass through his soul; but another will then hear the eternal language of the world-spirit, and for him are unveiled the mysteries of creation.

One must have learned to control one's own feelings and ideas if one wishes to develop any intimate relationship with the outer world. Every phenomenon in that outer world is full of divine splendor, but one must have felt the Divine within oneself before one may hope to discover it without. The disciple is told to set apart certain moments of his daily life during which to withdraw into himself, quietly and alone. At such times he ought not to occupy himself with his own personal affairs, for this would bring about the contrary of that at which he is aiming. During these moments he ought rather to listen in complete silence to the echoes of what he has experienced, of what the outward world has told him. Then, in these periods of quiet, every flower, every animal, every action will unveil to him secrets undreamed of, and thus will he prepare himself to receive new impressions of the external world, as if he viewed it with different eyes. For he who merely desires to enjoy impression after impression, only stultifies the perceptive faculty, while he who lets the enjoyment afterwards reveal something to him, thus enlarges and educates it. He must be careful not merely to let the enjoyment reverberate, as it were; but, renouncing any further emotions of joy, begin to work upon his pleasurable experiences with an inward activity. The danger at this point is very great. Instead of working within one-self, it is easy to fall into the opposite habit of afterward trying to completely exhaust the enjoyment. Let us not undervalue the unforeseen sources of error which here confront the disciple. He must of necessity pass through a host of temptations, each of which tends only to harden his Ego and to imprison it within itself. He ought to open it wide for the whole world. It is necessary that he should seek enjoyment, for in this way only can the outward world get at him; and if he blunts himself to enjoyment he becomes as a plant which cannot longer draw nourishment from its environment. Yet, if he stops at the enjoyment, he is then shut up within himself, and will only be something to himself and nothing to the world. However much he may live within himself, however intensely he may cultivate his Ego, the world will exclude him. He is dead to the world. The disciple considers enjoyment only as a means of ennobling himself for the world. Pleasure to him is as a scout who informs him concerning the world, and after having been taught by pleasure he passes on to work. He does not learn in order that he may accumulate wisdom as his own treasure, but in order that he may put his learning at the service of the world.

In all forms of Occultism there is a fundamental principle which must not be transgressed, if any goal at all is to be reached. All occult teachers must impress upon their pupils that, Every branch of knowledge which you seek only to enrich your own learning, only to accumulate treasure for yourself, leads you away from the Path; but all knowledge which you seek for working in the service of humanity and for the uplifting of the world brings you a step forward. This law must be rigidly observed; nor is one a genuine disciple until he has adopted it as the guide for his whole life. In many occult schools this truth is expressed in the following short sentence: Every idea which does not become an ideal for you, slays a power within your soul: every idea which becomes an ideal creates within you a vital force.

III

THE PATH OF DISCIPLESHIP

At the very beginning of his course the student is directed to the Path of Reverence, and the development of the inner life. The occult teaching also gives practical instructions by the observance of which he may learn to follow that Path and develop that inner life. These practical directions have no arbitrary basis. They rest on ancient experience and ancient wisdom, and wheresoever the ways to higher knowledge are marked out, they are of the same nature. All genuine teachers of Occultism agree as to the essential character of these rules, although they do not always express them in the same words. This difference of expression is of a minor character, more seeming than real, and is due to circumstances which need not be mentioned here.

No teacher wishes, by means of such rules, to establish an ascendency over other persons. He would not tamper with individual independence. Indeed, no one respects and cherishes human individuality more than the teachers of Occultism. It was said, in the first part of this book, that the order which embraces all Initiates was surrounded by a wall, and that two laws formed the principles by which it was upheld. Whenever the Initiate leaves this enclosure and steps forth into the world, he must submit to a third inviolable law. It is this: Keep watch over each of your actions and each of your words, in order that you may not hinder the free-will of any human being. Those who recognize that genuine occult teachers are thoroughly permeated with this principle will understand that they can add to their independence by the practical directions which they are advised to follow.

One of the first of these rules may be thus expressed in our language: "Provide for yourself moments of inward calm, and in these moments learn to distinguish between the real and the unreal." I say advisedly "expressed in our language," because originally all rules and teachings of occult science were expressed in a symbolical sign-language. Those who desire to master its whole scope and meaning must first obtain permission to learn this symbolical language, and before such permission may be obtained, it is necessary to have taken the first steps in occult knowledge. This may be achieved by the careful observance of such rules as are here given. The Path is open to all who earnestly will to enter it.

Simple, in truth and easy to follow, is the rule concerning moments of inner calm; but it leads to the goal only when the pursuit is as earnest and strict as the way is simple. It will, therefore, be stated here, without further preamble, the method in which this rule should be observed.

The student must mark off a small part of his daily life in which to occupy himself with something quite different from the avocations of his ordinary life, and the way in which he occupies himself at such a time must also differ from the way in which he performs the rest of his duties. But this does not mean that what he does in the time thus set apart has no connection with his daily work. On the contrary, the man who seeks such moments in the right way will soon find that it is just this which gives him full power to do his daily task. Nor must it be supposed that the observance of this rule really deprives anyone of time needed for the performance of his duties. If any person really has no more time at his disposal, five minutes a day will suffice. The real point is the manner in which these five minutes are spent.

At these periods a man should raise himself completely above his work-a-day life. His thoughts and feelings must take on a different coloring. His joys and sorrows, his cares, experiences, and actions, must pass in review before his soul. And he must cultivate a frame of mind which enables him to regard all his other experiences from a higher point of view. We need only bear in mind how different is the point of view from which in ordinary life we regard the experiences and actions of another, and that from which we judge our own. This is inevitable, for we are interwoven with our own actions and experiences, while we only contemplate those of another. Our aim, in moments of retirement, must be to contemplate and judge our own experiences and actions, as though it were not ourselves but some other person to whom they applied. Suppose, for example, that a certain misfortune has befallen someone. What a different attitude that person takes towards it as compared with an identical misfortune that has befallen his neighbor! No one can blame this attitude as unjustifiable; it is a part of human nature. And just as it is in exceptional circumstances, so it is also in the daily affairs of life. The student must endeavor to attain the power of regarding himself at certain times as he would regard a stranger. He must contemplate himself with the inward calm of the critic. When this is attained, our own experiences present themselves in a new light. As long as we are interwoven with them and are, as it were, within them, we are as closely connected with the unreal as with the real. When we attain to a calm survey, the real is separated from the unreal. Sorrow and joy, every thought, every resolve, appear changed when we contemplate ourselves in this way. It is as though we had spent the whole day in a place where we saw the smallest objects at the same range of vision as the largest ones, and in the evening climbed a neighboring hill and surveyed the whole scene at once. Then the parts of the place take on proportions different from those they bore when seen from within. The value of such calm inward contemplation depends less on the actual thing we contemplate than on the power which such inward calm develops in us.

For in every human being there is, besides what we call the work-a-day man, a higher being. This higher being remains concealed until it is awakened. And each of us can only awaken it for himself. But as long as this higher being is not awakened, the higher faculties that might lead to supersensual knowledge, must lie dormant or remain hidden in every man. This power which leads to inward calm is a magic force that sets free certain higher faculties. Until a seeker feels this magic force within him, he must continue to follow strictly and earnestly the rules given. To every man who thus perseveres, the day will come when a spiritual light is revealed to him, and a whole new world, whose existence was hitherto unsuspected, is discerned by an eye within him.

Because he begins to follow this rule, there is no need for any outward change in the life of the student. He performs his duties as before, and at first he endures the same sorrows and experiences the same joys as of old. In no way does it estrange him from life, rather is he enabled to devote himself to it the more completely, because in the moments set apart he has a Higher Life of his own. Gradually this Higher Life will make its influence felt on the ordinary life. The calm of the moments set apart will influence his ordinary existence as well. The whole man will grow calmer, will attain serenity in all his actions, and will cease to be perturbed by all manner of incidents. Gradually a student who thus advances will guide himself more and more, and be less governed by circumstances and external influences. Such a man will soon discover how great a source of strength lies for him in these periods of contemplation. He will cease to be annoyed by things that formerly worried him; and countless matters that once filled him with fear will now cease to alarm him. He acquires a new outlook on life. Formerly he may have taken up this or that task with a sense of timidity. He would say: "I lack the power to do this as well as I could wish." Now he no longer admits such a thought but, instead forms one quite different. He says to himself: "I will summon all my strength in order to do my work as well as I possibly can." And he suppresses the thought which encourages timidity; for he knows that this very timidity might spoil his undertaking, and that in any event it can contribute nothing to the improvement of his labor. And thus one thought after another, each fraught with advantage to his whole life, begins to penetrate the student's outlook. They take the place of those which gave a hampering and weakening effect. He begins to steer his own ship, on a firm, secure course, among the waves of life, which formerly tossed it helplessly to and fro.

And this calm and serenity react on the whole being. They assist the growth of the inner man, and of those inner faculties which lead to higher knowledge. For it is by his progress in this direction that the student gradually attains to a state in which he himself determines the manner in which the impressions of the external world shall affect him. Thus, he may hear a word, spoken with the object of wounding or vexing him. Before he began his occult studies it would indeed have been painful or irritating. But now that he is in the Path of Discipleship, he is able to take from it the sting or the power to hurt, even before it enters his consciousness. Take another example: we naturally grow impatient when we are kept waiting, but the student is so permeated, in his moments of calm, with the realization of the uselessness of impatience, that this calmness is present with him on every occasion. The impatience which would naturally overcome him vanishes, and an interval which would otherwise have been wasted in the expression of impatience may be utilized by making some profitable observation during the period of waiting.

Now we must realize the significance of these facts. We must remember that the "Higher Being" in a man is in constant development, and only the state of calm and serenity here described renders an orderly development possible. The waves of outward life press in upon the inner man from all sides, if, instead of controlling this outward life, he is controlled by it. Such a man is like a plant which tries to expand in a cleft in the rock, and is stunted in its growth until new space is given it. No outward forces can supply space for the inner man; it can only be supplied by the inner calm which he may give to his soul.

Outward circumstances can only alter the course of his outward life; they can never awaken the spiritual inner man. The student must himself give birth to the new and higher man within him.

The higher man becomes the "inner Ruler," who directs the circumstances of the outer man with sure guidance. As long as the latter has the upper hand, this inner man is enslaved, and cannot therefore develop his powers. If another than myself has the power to make me angry, I am not master of myself, or, to put it better, I have not yet found "the Ruler within me." I must develop the power within, of letting the impressions of the outer world approach me only in the way in which I myself choose; then only do I really become an occult student. And only by earnestly striving after this power can a student reach the goal. It is not of so much importance to achieve a great deal in a given time, as to be earnest in the search. Many have striven for years without noticing any marked advance; but many of those who did not despair, and struggled on undaunted, have sometimes quite suddenly achieved the "inner victory."

In many situations it requires a good deal of effort to achieve these moments of inward calm. But the greater the effort needed, the more important is the achievement. In esoteric studies, everything depends on the energy, inward truthfulness, and uncompromising sincerity with which we contemplate ourselves and our actions from the standpoint of complete strangers.

But only one side of the student's inner activity is characterized by this birth of his own higher being. Something else in addition is needed. Even if a man regards himself as a stranger, it is only himself that he contemplates; he looks at those experiences and actions, with which he is connected, through his particular mode of life, while it is necessary for him to rise above this, and attain to a purely human point of view, to be no longer connected with his own individual circumstances. He must pass on to the contemplation of those things which concern him as a human being, even though he dwell in a different condition and different circumstances. In this way something is brought to birth within him which rises beyond the personal point of view. Thus his gaze is directed to higher worlds than those he knows in every-day life. And then he begins to feel and realize that he belongs to these higher worlds about which his senses and his daily occupations can tell him nothing. In this way he shifts the central point of his being to the inner part of his nature. He listens to the voices within him which speak to him in his moments of calm; and inwardly he cultivates an intercourse with the spiritual world, which removes him from the every-day world, whose voices he no longer hears. Around him there is silence. He puts away from him all his external surroundings, and everything which even reminds him of such external impressions. His entire soul is filled with calm, inward contemplation and converse with the purely spiritual world. This calm contemplation must become a necessity to the student. He is plunged completely into a world of thought, and must develop an earnest desire for calm thinking. He must learn to love the in-pouring of the spirit. Then he will learn to regard this thought-world and its thought-forms as more real than the every-day things which surround him, and he begins to deal with thoughts as with things existing in space. And then the moment is at hand when the revelations of his quiet thinking begin to seem much higher and more real than the things existing in space. He discovers that this thought-world is an expression of life, and realizes that thoughts are not mere phantoms, but that through them, beings, who were hidden before, now speak to him. He begins to hear voices through the silence. Formerly his ear was the only organ of hearing; now he can listen with his soul. An inner language and an inner voice are revealed to him. It is a moment of supremest ecstasy to the student when this experience first comes to him. An inner light floods the whole external world for him, and he is "born anew." Through his being passes a current from a divine world, bringing with it divine bliss.

This thought-life of the soul, which is gradually widened into a life of spiritual being, is designated by the Gnosis and by Theosophy as meditation (contemplative thought). This meditation is the means by which supersensual knowledge is attained. But during such moments the student must not be content to give himself up to the luxury of sensation. He must not permit undefined feelings to take possession of his soul. That would only hinder him from attaining true spiritual knowledge. His thoughts must be clearly and sharply defined, and he will be helped in this by not allowing himself to be carried away blindly by the thoughts that spring up within him. Rather must he permeate his mind with the lofty ideas which originated with advanced students to whom inspiration has already come. Let him first of all study the wisdom which originated in such moments of meditation. The student will find such in the mystical, gnostic, and theosophical literature of our time, and will there gain the material for his meditation. Wise men have inscribed in these books the thoughts of divine science, or have proclaimed them to the world through their agents.

Such meditation produces a complete transformation in the student. He begins to form entirely new conceptions of Reality. All things acquire fresh values in his eyes. And it cannot be declared too often that this transformation does not estrange him from the world nor keep him from his daily round of duties. For he begins to realize that his most insignificant actions or experiences are in close connection with the great cosmic beings and events. When once this connection is revealed to him in his moments of contemplation, he is endowed with fresher and fuller power for his daily duties. For then he knows that his labor and his suffering are given and endured for the sake of a great spiritual cosmic whole. Thus, instead of weariness, his meditation gives him strength to live.

With firm step the student advances in life. No matter what it may bring him, he goes forward erect. In the past he knew not why he worked and suffered, but now he knows. It is obvious that such meditation is more likely to lead to the goal, if conducted under the direction of experienced persons, who know actually how everything may best be done. We should, therefore, seek the advice and direction of such experienced guides (they are called Gurus in certain schools of thought). What would otherwise be mere uncertain groping is transformed by such direction into work that is sure of its goal. Those who apply to the teachers having such knowledge and experience will never apply in vain. They must, however, be quite sure that it is the advice of a friend they desire, not the domination of a would-be ruler. Those who really know are always the most modest of men, and nothing is further from their nature than what is called the passion for power.

Those who, by means of meditation, rise to that which unites man with spirit, are bringing to life within them the eternal element which is not limited by birth nor death. Only those who have had no experience for themselves can doubt the existence of this eternal element. Thus meditation becomes the way by which man also attains to the recognition and contemplation of his eternal, indestructible, essential being. And only through meditation can one attain to such a view of life. Gnosis and Theosophy tell of the eternal nature of this essential being, and of its reincarnation. The question is often asked: "Why does a man know nothing of those experiences which lie beyond the borders of birth and death?" Not thus should we ask, but rather: "How may we attain to such knowledge?" The entrance to the Path is opened by right meditation. This alone can revive the memory of events that lie beyond the borders of birth and death. Everyone can attain to this knowledge; in each of us is the faculty of recognizing and contemplating for ourselves the truths of Mysticism, Theosophy, and Gnosis; but the right means must be chosen. Only a being with ears and eyes can perceive tones and colors, nor can the eye perceive without the light by which things are made visible. Occult science gives the means of developing the spiritual ears and eyes, and kindling the spiritual light. There are, according to esoteric teachers, three steps by which the goal may be attained: 1. Probation. This develops the spiritual senses. 2. Enlightenment. This kindles the spiritual light. 3. Initiation. This establishes intercourse with the higher spiritual beings.

The following teachings proceed from a secret tradition, but precise information concerning its nature and its name cannot be given at present. They refer to the three steps which, in the school of this tradition, lead to a certain degree of initiation. But here we shall find only so much of this tradition as may be openly declared. These teachings are extracted from a much deeper and more secret doctrine. In the occult schools themselves a definite course of instruction is followed, and in addition to this there are certain practices which enable the souls of men to attain a conscious intercourse with the spiritual world. These practices bear about the same relation to what will be imparted in the following pages, as the teaching which is given in a well-disciplined school bears to the instruction that may be received occasionally during a walk. And yet the ardent and persevering search for what is here hinted at will lead to the way by which one obtains access to a genuine occult school. But, of course, an impatient perusal, devoid of sincerity and perseverance, can lead to nothing at all. He who believes himself to be ready for more must apply to an occult teacher. The study of these things can only be successful if the student will observe what has already been written in previous chapters.

The stages which the above-mentioned tradition specifies are the following three:

I. Probation,
II. Enlightenment,
III. Initiation.

It is not altogether necessary that these three stages should be so taken that one must have quite completed the first before beginning the second, nor this in its turn before commencing the third. With respect to certain things one can partake of

Enlightenment, and even of Initiation, while with others one is still in the probationary stage. Yet it will be necessary to spend a certain time in this stage of Probation before any Enlightenment at all can commence, and at least to some degree one must be enlightened before it is possible even to enter upon the stage of Initiation. In giving an account of them, however, it is necessary, for the sake of clearness, that the three stages follow, one after another.

IV

PROBATION

Probation consists of a strict cultivation of the emotional and mental life. Through this cultivation the "spiritual body" becomes equipped with new instruments of perception and new organs of activity, just as, out of indeterminate living matter, the natural forces have fitted the physical body with the various organs so well known to the physical senses.

The beginning of this cultivation is made by directing the attention of the soul to certain events in the world that surrounds us. Such events are the germinating, expanding, and flourishing of life in its myriad forms on the one hand, and, on the other, the fading, decaying, and passing out of life from all things so far as perceptible to the ordinary senses. Wherever we turn our eyes we can observe these things happening simultaneously, and everywhere they naturally evoke in men thoughts and feelings. But under ordinary circumstances a man fails to grasp the importance of these sensations. He hurries on too quickly from impression to impression. What is necessary, therefore, is that he should fix his attention intently and quite consciously upon these phenomena. Wherever he observes expansion and flourishing of a certain kind, he must banish everything else from his soul, and entirely surrender himself for a short time to this one impression. He will soon convince himself that a sensation which heretofore in a similar case would have merely flitted through his soul, is now so magnified that it becomes of a powerful and energetic nature. He should at once allow this thought-form to reverberate throughout his whole being, yet quietly within himself, and to do so he must become inwardly quite still. He should draw himself away from the outward world, and follow only that which his soul tells him.

Yet it must not be thought that we can make much progress if we blunt our senses to the world. For, one must first contemplate these objects as keenly and precisely as possible, and then give up to the sensations that result, and the thoughts that arise within the soul. What is most important is, that one should direct the attention, with perfect inner balance, upon both of these phenomena. If one obtains the necessary quiet and surrenders himself to that which arises in the soul, he will, in due time, experience many wonderful thoughts and feelings, unknown to him before. Indeed, the more one fixes the attention in such a way, alternately upon something growing, expanding, and flourishing, and upon something else that is fading and decaying, the more vivid will these feelings become. And just as natural forces evolve the physical eyes and ears of the physical body, out of living matter, so will the organs of clairvoyance evolve themselves from the spiritual feelings which are thus evoked. A definite thought-form unites itself with the germinating and expanding object, and another, equally definite, with that which is fading and decaying. But this will only take place if the cultivation of these feelings be striven for in the way described.

It is possible to describe only approximately what these feelings are like. Indeed, everyone must arrive at his own conception of them as he passes through these inward experiences. He who has frequently fixes his attention on the phenomena of germinating, expanding, and flourishing, will feel something remotely allied to the sensation caused by witnessing a sunrise; and the phenomena of fading and decaying will produce in him an experience comparable, in the same way, to the gradual uprising of the moon on the horizon. Both these feelings are forces which, when carefully cultivated, with a continually increasing improvement, will lead to the greatest occult results. To him who again and again, systematically and with design, surrenders himself to such feelings, a new world is opened. The "Spiritual" world, the so-called "Astral plane," begins to dawn upon him. Blooming and fading are facts which no longer make indefinite impressions on him, as of old, but instead they form themselves into spiritual lines and figures of which he had previously suspected nothing. And these lines and figures have for the different phenomena different forms. A blooming flower, an animal growing, a decaying tree, evoke in his soul definite lines. The astral plane slowly broadens out before him. Its forms are not in any sense arbitrary. For two students who find themselves at the same stage of development will always see the same lines and figures under the same conditions. Just as certainly as a round table will be seen as round by two normal persons, not as round by the one and square by the other; so, too, before the perception of two souls a blooming flower will present the same spiritual form. And just as the shapes of animals and plants are described in ordinary natural history, so, too, the teacher in an occult school describes and delineates the spiritual forms of growing and decaying processes after their nature and species.

If the student has progressed so far that he can see such aspects of phenomena which are also physically observable with his external eyes, he will then be not far from the condition which will enable him to behold things that have no physical existence, and must therefore remain entirely hidden to those who have undergone no training in an occult school.

It should be emphasized that the occult explorer ought never to lose himself in speculation on the meaning of this or that. By such intellectualizing he only directs himself away from the right road. He ought to look out on the sense-world freshly, with healthy senses and quickened observation, and then to give himself up to his own sensations. He ought not to wish, in a speculative manner, to make out what this or that means, but rather to allow the things themselves to inform him.[6]

A further point of importance is that which is called in occult science "orientation in the higher worlds." This point is attained when one realizes with complete consciousness that feelings and thoughts are veritable realities, just as much as are tables and chairs in the world of the physical senses. Feelings and thoughts act upon each other in the astral-world and in the thought (or mental) world, just as objects of sense act upon each other in the physical world. As long as anyone is not truly permeated with this realization, he will not believe that an evil thought projected from his mind may have as devastating an effect upon other thought forms as that wrought upon physical objects by a bullet

---

[6] It should be remarked that artistic perception, when coupled with a quiet introspective nature, forms the best foundation for the development of occult faculties. It pierces through the superficial aspect of things and in so doing touches their secrets.

shot at random. Such a one will perhaps never allow himself to perform a physically visible action which he considers to be wrong, yet he will not shrink from harboring evil thoughts or feelings, for these do not appear to him to be dangerous to the rest of the world. Nevertheless we can advance in occult science only when we guard our thoughts and feelings in just the same way as a man would guard the steps he takes in the physical world. If anyone sees a wall before him he does not attempt to dash right through it, but directs his course alongside; in other words, he guides himself by the laws of the physical world.

There are such laws also in the world of thought and feeling, but there they cannot impose themselves upon us from without. They must flow out of the life of the soul itself. We arrive at such a condition when we forbid ourselves, at all times, to foster wrong thoughts or feelings. All arbitrary goings to-and-fro, all idle fancies, all accidental ups-and-downs of emotion must be forbidden in the same way. But, in so doing, let it not be thought that we bring about a deficiency of emotion. On the contrary, if we regulate our inner life in this manner, we shall speedily find ourselves rich in feelings and in genuine creative imagination. In place of a mere chaos of petty feelings and fantastic trains of thought, there appear significant emotions, and thoughts that are fruitful, and it is emotions and thoughts of this kind that lead a man to "orientation in the higher world." He has entered into the right condition for the things of that world, and they entail for him definite consequences. Just as a physical man finds his way between physical things, so, too, his path now leads him straight between the growing and the fading, which he has already come to know in the way described above. For he follows all processes of growing and flourishing, (and, on the other hand, of withering and decaying) that is necessary for his own and the world's prosperity.

The occult student has also to bestow a further care on the world of sound. He must discriminate between the tones which are produced from the so-called inert (lifeless) bodies (for example, a bell, a musical instrument, or a falling mass), and those which proceed from a living creature (an animal or a person). He who hears the striking of a bell will receive the sound and attach to it a certain sensation, but he who hears the cry of an animal will, in addition to this sensation, become aware that the sound reveals also an inward experience of the animal, either of pain or of pleasure. The student is concerned with the latter aspect of the sound. He must concentrate his whole attention upon it, so that the sound reveals to him something that lies outside of his own soul, and, more than this, must merge himself in this exterior thing. He must closely connect his own emotion with the pleasure or pain communicated to him by means of the sound, and must care nothing whether the sound be pleasant or unpleasant to him, welcome or not; his soul must be filled with only that which proceeds from the creature out of whom the sound has come. He who systematically and deliberately performs such exercises will develop within himself the faculty of intermingling, as it were, with the creature from which the sound proceeded. A person sensitive to music will find it easier to cultivate his spiritual life in this respect than one who is unmusical, but no one should think that a mere sense of music will take the place of this culture.

As an occult student, one must learn to contemplate the whole of nature in this way. By so doing a new faculty is developed in the world of thought and feeling. Through her manifold sounds the whole of Nature begins to whisper secrets to the student. What hitherto was merely incomprehensible noise to his soul will become by this means a coherent language of Nature. And whereas, hitherto, he heard sound only from the resonance of so-called inanimate objects, he now understands a new speech of the soul. Should he advance in this culture of the soul, he will soon learn that he can hear what hitherto he did not even surmise. He begins to hear with the soul.

One thing more must be added before we can reach the topmost point in this direction. What is of special importance in the development of the student is the way in which he hears the speech of other men. He must accustom himself to do this in such a way that while doing so his inner self is absolutely still. If someone expresses an opinion and another hears it, the inner self of the latter will be stirring in general assent or contradiction. Many people in such a case feel themselves urged to an expression of their assent, or, more especially, of their contradiction. All such assent or contradiction must, in the occult student, be silenced. It is not imperative that he should, therefore, quite suddenly begin to make his life entirely different, in order that he may attain to this inward and fundamental calm. He might, therefore, begin by doing so in special cases, deliberately selected by himself. Thus quite slowly and by degrees will this new way of listening creep into his habits, as of itself: In the occult schools these things are systematically practiced. For the sake of practice the student is obliged to listen for a certain period to the most contradictory thoughts, and at the same time to suppress all assent, and more especially all adverse criticism. The point is that in such a way not only all intellectual judgment is silenced, but also all sense of displeasure, denial, or even acceptance. The student must be particularly watchful that such feelings, even if they are not upon the surface, do not still remain lurking in the innermost recesses of his soul. He must listen, for example, to the statements of people who in some respects are far beneath him, and, while so doing, suppress every feeling of greater knowledge or of superiority. It is useful for everyone to listen in this way to children, for even the wisest may learn very much from children. So does it come about that we hear the words of others impersonally, completely divested of our own personality with its opinions and feelings. He who thus makes a practice of listening uncritically, even when a completely contradictory opinion is advanced, learns again and again to blend himself, to become identified, with the being of another. He then hears, as it were, through the words and into the souls of others. Through continual exercise of this kind only, sound becomes the right medium for the revelation of the spirit and the soul. Of course, it implies the strictest self-discipline, but it leads to a high goal. When these practices are undertaken in connection with those that deal with the sounds of Nature, the soul develops a new sense of hearing. It is enabled to receive demonstrations from the spiritual world which do not find their expression in outward sounds apprehensible by the physical ear. The perception of the "inner word" awakens. Gradually truths from the spiritual world reveal themselves to the student, and he hears them expressed in a spiritual way.[7]

---

[7] Only to him, who listens disinterestedly, comes the ability to perceive

All high truths are attained through such "inner encouragement," and what we hear from the lips of a genuine occult teacher has been experienced in this manner. In so saying it must not be supposed that it is useless to acquaint oneself with the writings on occult science, before one can actually gain this inner encouragement. On the contrary, the reading of such writings, and the listening to eminent teachers of occult lore, are themselves the means of attaining a personal knowledge. Every sentence of the esoteric wisdom which one hears is adapted to direct the senses to that point which must be attained before the soul can experience a real advance. To the practice of all that has been indicated, must be added an ardent study of what the occult teacher gives out to the world. In all occult schools such a study belongs to the probationary period, and he who would employ other methods will attain no goal if he omits the instructions of the occult teacher, for inasmuch as these instructions proceed from an actual "inner word," an actual "encouragement," they possess in themselves a spiritual vitality. They are not mere words; they are living powers; and while you follow the words of an occultist, while you read a book which comes from a genuine inner experience, powers are at work in your soul which make you clairvoyant, just as natural forces have created out of living matter your eyes and ears.

---

really from within, silently, and without emotion arising from personal opinion or personal taste,—to such only can the Great Souls, who are known in Occultism as the Masters speak. As long as our opinions and feelings are in a state of vehement opposition to the communications from the Masters, They remain silent.

V

ENLIGHTENMENT

Enlightenment is the result of very simple processes. Here, too, it is a matter of developing certain feelings and thoughts which are dormant within all men, but must be awakened. Only he who carries out these simple processes with complete patience, continuously and strenuously, can be led by them to the reception of inner illumination. The primary step is taken by observing in a particular way different natural objects—a transparent stone of beautiful form (a crystal), a plant, and an animal. One should endeavor at first to direct one's whole attention to a comparison of the stone with the animal, as follows: The thoughts which, accompanied by strong emotions, are thus induced, must pass through the soul, and no other emotions or thoughts must be mixed with them, or disturb the intense contemplation. One then says to oneself: "The stone has a form and the animal also has a form. The stone remains motionless in its place, but the animal is able to move about. It is impulse (desire) which causes the animal to change its place, and it is these impulses to which the form of the animal is of use. Its organs and instruments are the expression of these impulses. The form of the stone, on the contrary, is fashioned, not in accordance with impulses, but in accordance with an impulseless force."[8]

---

[8] The fact here mentioned, in its bearing on the contemplation of crystals, is in many ways distorted by those who have only heard of it

If one sinks deeply into such thoughts, and while so doing observes the stone and the animal with fixed attention, then there arise in the soul two separate kinds of emotion. From the stone into the soul there streams one kind of emotion, and from the animal, another. Probably in the beginning the experiment will not succeed, but little by little, with genuine and patient practice, these emotions become manifest. Again and again one should practice. At first the emotions last only as long as the contemplation. Later on, they work afterwards, and then they grow to something which remains alive in the soul. One then needs only to reflect, and both emotions invariably arise, apart from all contemplation of an external object.

Out of these emotions, and the thoughts which are bound up with them, clairvoyant organs are formed. Should the plant be added to the contemplation, one will notice that the feeling outflowing from it, both in its quality and in its degree, lies between that which emanates from the stone and that from the animal. The organs which are so formed are spiritual eyes. We learn by degrees and through their means to see both astral and mental colors. As long as one has attained only the condition described as Probation, the spiritual world with its lines and figures remains dark, but through Enlightenment it will become clear. It must be noted here that the words "dark" and "light," as well as the other common expressions, only approximately describe what is really meant; for language as usually understood is constructed to suit physical conditions alone.

---

in an outward (exoteric) manner, and in this way such practises as crystal-gazing have their origin. Misrepresentations of such a kind are the outcome of misunderstanding. They have been described in many books, but they never form the subject of genuine (esoteric) teaching.

Occult science describes what emanates from the stone and is seen by clairvoyant eyes, as "blue" or "bluish-red," and that which is observed as coming from the animal is described as "red" or "reddish-yellow." In reality they are colors of a spiritual kind which are discerned. The color proceeding from the plant is "green." Plants are just those natural phenomena whose qualities in the higher worlds are similar to their qualities in the physical world, but it is not so with stones and animals. It must now be clearly understood that the above-mentioned colors only suggest the prevailing shades of the stone, the plant, or the animal. In reality, all possible overtones exist, for every animal, every stone, every plant has its own peculiar shade of color. In addition to these there are the creatures of the higher worlds, who always incorporate themselves with colors not their own, often marvellous, often horrible. In short, the variety of colors in these higher worlds is immeasurably greater than in the physical world.

If a man has once acquired the faculty of seeing with spiritual eyes, he sooner or later, meets with the beings here mentioned, some of them higher, some lower than man himself; beings who never entered into physical existence.

When he has advanced thus far, the way to a great deal lies open before him; but it is inadvisable to proceed further without an experienced guide. Indeed, for all that has here been described, such experienced guidance is desirable, and he who has the endurance to fulfil the elementary conditions of enlightenment, will assuredly seek and discover his guide.

Under all circumstances it is important to give warning, and he who will not heed it had better leave untrodden all the steps of occult science. It is necessary that he who would become an occult student should lose none of his attributes as a good and noble man, and one susceptible to all physical truths. Indeed, throughout his apprenticeship he must continually increase his moral strength, his inner purity, and his powers of observation. Let us give an example: During the preliminary practices of Enlightenment, the student must be careful always to be enlarging his sympathy with the animal and human worlds, and his sense of nature's beauty. If he is not careful to do this he continually dulls both sense and feeling; his heart grows cold and his sympathies dwarfed; which lead to perilous results.

How enlightenment proceeds, in the sense of the foregoing practices, if one rises from the stone, the plant, and the animal, up to man, and how, after enlightenment, under all circumstances, the gentle hand of the Pilot comes on a certain day, and leads to Initiation—of these things the next chapter will deal in so far as it can and may do so.

In our time, the path to occult science is sought after by many. It is sought in various ways, and many dangerous and even objectionable modes are practiced. Therefore it is that those who know of the truth and dangers concerning these things have allowed a greater portion of the occult training and the necessary warning to be published. Only so much is here imparted as this permission allows, and it is necessary that something of the truth should be known in order that it may counteract the great danger of these errors. If nothing be forced, there is no danger for him who follows the way already described; only one thing should be noted: no one ought to spend more time or power upon such practices than is at his disposal with due regard to his circumstances and his duties. No one ought suddenly to change anything in the external conditions of his life. If one desires genuine results, one must have patience; one should be able to cease the practice after a few minutes, and then peacefully to continue one's daily work, and no thought of these practices ought to be mingled with the work of the day. He who has not learned to wait, in the best and highest sense of the word, is of no use as an occult student, nor will he ever attain results of much real value.

He who is in search of occult knowledge, by the means indicated in the foregoing pages, must fortify himself throughout the whole course of his efforts by the understanding that after persevering for some time he may have made suitable progress without becoming conscious of it in the precise way which he had expected. He who does not remember this is likely to lose heart, and in a little while to abandon his efforts altogether. The mental powers and faculties about to be developed are at first of the most subtle kind, and their nature differs entirely from the conceptions of them which may be formed in the student's mind. He has been accustomed to occupy himself with the physical world alone, and the mental and astral worlds seem to elude his gaze, and baffle his conceptions. It is, therefore, not remarkable if, at first, he fails to realize the new forces, mental and astral, which are developing in his own being. This is why it is dangerous to enter the path leading to occult knowledge without experienced guidance. The teacher can see the progress made by the pupil, long before the latter becomes conscious of it for himself. He sees the delicate organs of spiritual vision beginning to form themselves, before the pupil is aware of their existence, and a great part of the duties of the teacher consists in perpetual watchfulness, lest the disciple lose confidence, patience, and perseverance, before he becomes conscious of his own progress. The teacher, as we know, can confer upon the student no powers which are not already latent within him, and his sole function is to assist in the awakening of slumbering faculties. But he may be a pillar of strength to him who strives to penetrate through darkness into the light.

There are many who leave the occult path soon after setting foot upon it, because they are not immediately conscious of their own progress. And even when higher experiences begin to dawn upon the seeker, he is apt to regard them as illusions, because he had anticipated them quite differently. He loses courage, either because he regards these first experiences as of no value, or because they appear so insignificant that he has no hope of their leading to any appreciable results within a measurable time. Courage and self-confidence are the two lamps which must never be allowed to burn themselves out on the pathway to the occult. He who cannot patiently repeat an exercise which has failed for an apparently unlimited number of times, will never travel far.

Long before one is aware of any distinct perception of progress, comes an inarticulate mental impression that the right road has been found. This is a feeling to be welcomed, and to be encouraged, since it may evolve into a trustworthy guide. Above all, it is imperative to extirpate the idea that any fantastic, mysterious practices are required for the attainment of higher experiences. It must be clearly realized that ordinary every-day human feelings and thoughts must form the basis from which the start is to be made, and that it is only needful to give these thoughts and feelings a new direction. Everyone must say to himself: "In my own sphere of thoughts and sensations lie enfolded the deepest mysteries, but hitherto I have been unable to perceive them." In the end it all resolves itself into the fact that man, ordinarily, carries body, soul and spirit about with him, yet is conscious only of the body, not of the soul and spirit, and that the student in due time attains to a similar consciousness of soul and spirit.

Hence it is highly important to give the proper direction to thoughts and feelings, in order that one may develop the perception of that which is invisible to a person living the ordinary life. One of the ways by which this development may be carried out will now be indicated. Again, like almost everything else we have explained so far, it is quite a simple matter. Yet the results are of the greatest consequence, if the experiment is carried out with perseverance, and in the right frame of mind.

Place before you the small seed of a plant. It is then necessary, while contemplating this significant object, to create with intensity the right kind of thoughts, and through these thoughts to develop certain feelings. In the first place, let the student clearly grasp what is really presented to his vision. Let him describe to himself the shape, color, and all other qualities of the grain of seed. Then let his mind dwell upon the following train of thought: "This grain of seed, if planted in the soil, will grow into a plant of complex structure." Let him clearly picture this plant to himself. Let him build it up in his imagination. And then let him reflect that the object now existing only in his imagination will presently be brought into actual physical existence by the forces of the earth and of light. If the thing contemplated by him were an artificially-made object, though such a close imitation of nature that no external difference could be detected by human eyesight, no forces inherent in the earth or light could avail to produce from it a plant. He who thoroughly grasps this thought and inwardly assimilates it will also be able to form the following idea with the right feeling. He will reasons thus: "That which is ultimately to grow out of this seed is already, as a force, now secretly enfolded within it. The artificial duplicate of the seed contains no such force. And yet both appear to be alike to my eyes. The real seed, therefore, contains something invisible which is not present in the imitation." It is this invisible something on which thought and feeling are now to be concentrated.[9] Let the student fully realize that this invisible something will later on translate itself into a visible plant, perceptible by him in shape and color. Let him dwell upon the thought: "The invisible will become visible. If I could not think, then I could not now realize, that which will become visible later on."

Particular stress must be laid on the importance of feeling with intensity that which one thinks. In calmness of mind a single thought must be vitally experienced within oneself to the exclusion of all disturbing influences. Sufficient time must be

---

[9] Anyone who might object that a microscopical examination would reveal the difference between the two would only show that he has failed to grasp the intention of the experiment. The intention is not to investigate the physical structure of the object, but to use it as a means for the development of psychic force.

taken to allow the thought, and the state of feeling connected therewith, to become, as it were, imbedded in the soul. If that is accomplished in the right way—possibly not until after numerous attempts—an inward force will make itself felt. And this force will create new powers of perception. The grain of seed will appear as if enclosed in a small luminous cloud. The spiritualized vision of the student perceives it as a kind of flame. This flame is of a lilac color in the centre, blue at the edges. Then appears that which one could not see before, and which was created by the power of thought and feeling brought into life within oneself. That which was physically invisible (the plant which will not become visible until later on) has there revealed itself to the spiritual eye.

It is pardonable if, to many men, all this appears to be mere illusion. Many will say: "What is the value of such visions or such hallucinations?" And many will thus fall away, and no longer continue to tread the path. But this is precisely the important point—not to confuse, at this difficult stage of human evolution, spiritual reality with the mere creations of phantasy, and to have the courage to press manfully onward, instead of growing timorous and faint-hearted. On the other hand, however, it is necessary to insist on the necessity of maintaining unimpaired, and of perpetually cultivating, the healthy attitude of mind which is required for the distinguishing of truth from illusion. Never during all these exercises must the student surrender the fully conscious control of himself. He must continue to think as soundly and sanely in these spiritual conditions as he does with regard to the things and occurrences of ordinary life. It would be unfortunate if he lapses into reveries. He must at every moment be clear-headed and sober-minded and it would be the greatest mistake if the student, through such practices, lost his mental equilibrium, or if he were prevented from judging as sanely and clearly as before, the matters of work-a-day life. The disciple should, therefore, examine himself again and again to find out whether he has remained unaltered in relation to the circumstances among which he lives, or whether perchance he has lost his mental balance. He must ever maintain a calm repose within his own individuality, and an open mind for everything, being careful at the same time not to drift into vague reveries or to experiment with all sorts of exercises.

The lines for development here indicated, belong to those which have been followed, and whose efficacy has been demonstrated in the schools of occultism from the earliest ages, and none but such will here be given. Anyone attempting to employ methods of meditation devised by himself, or which he may have come across in the course of promiscuous reading will inevitably be led astray, and will lose himself in a boundless morass of incoherent phantasies.

A further exercise which may succeed the one described above, is the following: Let the disciple place himself in front of a plant which has attained the stage of full development. Now let his mind be absorbed by the reflection that the time is near at hand when this plant will wither and die. "Nothing," he should say to himself, "nothing of what I now see before me will endure. But this plant will have evolved seeds which in their turn will grow into new plants. Again I become aware that in what I see something lies concealed which I cannot see. I will fill my mind wholly with the thought that this plant-form with its colors will cease to be. But the reflection that the plant has produced seeds teaches me that it will not disappear into nothing. That which will prevent this disappearance, I can at present no more see with my eyes than I could originally discern the plant in the grain of seed. The plant, therefore, contains something which my eyes are unable to see. If this thought fully lives in me, and combines with the corresponding state of feeling, then, in due time, there will again develop a force in my soul which will ripen into a new kind of perception." Out of the plant there grows once more a flame-like appearance, which is, of course, correspondingly larger than that which was previously described. This flame is greenish at the centre, and is tinged with yellow at the outer edge.

He who has won this vision has gained greatly, inasmuch as he sees things, not only in their present state of being, but also in their development and decay. He begins to see in all things the spirit, of which the bodily organs of sight have no perception, and he has taken the initial steps on that road, which will gradually lead him to the solution, by direct vision, of the secret of birth and death. To the outer senses, a being begins to exist at its birth, and ceases to exist at its death. This, however, only appears to be so, because these senses are unable to apprehend the concealed spirit. Birth and death are only, for this spirit, transformations, just as the unfolding of the flower from the bud is a transformation enacted before our physical eyes. But if one desires to attain to direct perception of these facts, one must first awaken the spiritual vision by the means here indicated.

In order to meet an objection which may be raised by certain people already possessed of some psychical experience, let it be at once admitted that there are shorter ways than this, and that there are persons who have direct perception of the actualities of birth and death, without having had to pass through all the stages of discipline here set forth. There are also human beings endowed with high psychical faculties, to whom only a slight impulse is necessary for the developing of these powers. But they are exceptional, and the methods described above are safer, and are capable of general application. Similarly, it is possible to gain some knowledge of chemistry by special methods; but in order to make safer the science of chemistry, the recognized, reliable course must be followed.

An error fraught with serious consequences would result from the assumption that the goal could be reached more simply by allowing the mind to dwell merely on an imaginary plant or a grain of seed. It may be possible by such means to evoke a force which would enable the soul to attain the inner vision. But this vision will be, in most cases, a mere figment of the imagination, for the main object is not to create arbitrarily a mental vision, but to allow the veritable nature of things to form an image within one's mind. The truth must come up from the depth of one's own soul, not at the call of one's ordinary self, but rather must the objects of one's perception themselves exercise their magical power, if one is to perceive their inner reality.

After the disciple has evolved, by such means, the rudiments of spiritual vision, he may proceed to the contemplation of human nature itself. Simple appearances of ordinary life must be chosen first. But before making any attempts in this direction, it is imperative for the student to strive after an absolute sincerity of moral character. He must banish all thoughts of ever using the insight to be attained in these ways for his own selfish ends. He must be absolutely determined that under no circumstances will he avail himself, in an evil sense, of any power which he may gain over his fellow-creatures. This is the reason why everyone who desires to gain direct insight into the secrets of human nature must follow the golden rule of true Occultism. And the golden rule is this: For every one step that you take in the pursuit of the hidden knowledge, take three steps in the perfecting of your own character. He who obeys this rule can perform such exercises as that which is now to be explained.

Begin by observing a person filled with a desire for some object. Direct your attention to this desire. It is best to choose a time when this desire is at its height, and when it is not yet certain whether the object of the desire will be attained or not. Then surrender yourself entirely to the contemplation of that which you observe, but maintain the utmost inner tranquility of soul. Make every endeavor to be deaf and blind to everything that may be going on around you at the same time, and bear in mind particularly that this contemplation is to evoke a state of feeling in your soul. Allow this state of feeling to arise in your soul, like a cloud rising on an otherwise cloudless horizon. It is to be expected, of course, that your observation will be interrupted, because the person on whom it is directed will not remain in this particular state of mind for a sufficient length of time. Presumably you will fail in your experiment hundreds and hundreds of times. It is simply a question of not losing patience. After many attempts you will ultimately realize the state of feeling spoken of above as fast as the corresponding mental phenomena pass through the soul of the person under observation. After a time you will begin to notice that this feeling in your own soul is evoking the power of spiritual vision into the psychical condition of the other. A luminous image will appear in your field of vision. And this luminous image is the so-called astral manifestation evoked by the desire-state when under observation. Again we may describe this image as flame-like in appearance. It is yellowish red in the centre and reddish-blue or lilac at the edges. Much depends upon treating such experiences of the inner vision with great delicacy. It will be best for you at first to talk of them to nobody except your teacher, if you have one. The attempt to describe such appearances in appropriate words usually leads to gross self-deception. One employs ordinary terms not applicable to such purposes, and therefore much too gross and clumsy. The consequence is that one's own attempt to clothe this vision in words unconsciously leads one to blend the actual experience with an alloy of imaginary details. It is, therefore, another important law for the occult inquirer that he should know how to observe silence concerning his inner visions. Observe silence even towards yourself. Do not endeavor to express in words that which you see, or to fathom it with reasoning faculties that are inadequate. Freely surrender yourself to these spiritual impressions without any mental reservations, and without disturbing them by thinking about them too much. For you must remember that your reasoning faculties were, at first, by no means equal to your faculties of observation. You have acquired these reasoning faculties through experiences hitherto confined exclusively to the world as apprehended by your physical senses, and the faculties you are now acquiring transcend these experiences. Do not, therefore, try to measure your new and higher perceptions by the old standard. Only he who has already gained some certainty in his observation of inner experiences ought to speak about them with the idea of thereby stimulating his fellow-beings.

As a supplementary exercise the following may be set forth. Direct your observation in the same way upon a fellow-being to whom the fulfilment of some wish, the gratification of some desire has just been granted. If the same rules and precautions are adopted as in the previous instance, you will once more attain to spiritual perception. You will distinguish a flame-like appearance which is yellow in the centre and greenish at the edges. By such observations of one's fellow-creatures one may easily be led into a moral fault—one may become uncharitable. All conceivable means must be taken to fight against this tendency. Anyone exercising such powers of observation should have risen to the level on which one is absolutely convinced that thoughts are actual things. He may then no longer allow himself to admit thoughts incompatible with the highest reverence for the dignity of human life and of human liberty. Not for one moment must he entertain the idea of regarding a human being as a mere object for observation. It must be the aim of self-education to see that the faculties for a psychic observation of human nature go hand in hand with a full recognition of the rights of each individual. That which dwells in each human being must be regarded as something holy, and to be held inviolate by us even in our thoughts and feelings. We must be possessed by a feeling of reverential awe for all that is human.

For the present, only these two examples can be given as to the methods by which an insight into human nature may be achieved, but they will at least serve to point out the way which must be followed. He who has gained the inner tranquility and repose which are indispensable for such observations, will by so doing, already have undergone a great transformation. This will soon reach the point at which the increase of his spiritual worth will manifest itself in the confidence and composure of his outward demeanor. Again, this alteration in his demeanor will react favorably on his inner condition, and thus he will be able to help himself further along the road. He will find ways of penetrating further and further into those secrets of human nature, those hidden from our external senses, and will then become qualified for a deeper insight into the mysterious correlations between the nature of man, and all else that exists in the universe. By following this path, the disciple will approach closer and closer to the day on which he will be deemed worthy of taking the first steps of initiation; but before these can be taken it is necessary to assure oneself of unflinching courage. At first it may not be at all apparent to the student why it should be necessary, but he cannot fail to be convinced of it in the end.

The quality which is indispensable to him who would be initiated is a certain measure of courage and fearlessness. He must absolutely go out of his way to find opportunities for developing these virtues. In the occult schools they are cultivated quite systematically; but life in this respect is itself an excellent school of occultism, nay, possibly the best. To face danger calmly, to try to overcome difficulties unswervingly, this is what the student must learn to do; for instance, in the presence of some peril, he must rise at once to the conception that fears are altogether useless, and ought not to be entertained for one moment, but that the mind ought simply to be concentrated on what is to be done. He must reach a point where it has become impossible for him ever again to feel afraid or to lose his courage. By self-discipline in this direction he will develop within himself distinct qualities which he needs if he is to be initiated into the higher mysteries. Just as man in his physical being requires nervous force in order to use his physical senses, so also, in his psychic nature, he requires the force which is only produced in the courageous and the fearless. For in penetrating to the higher mysteries he will see things not yet revealed to the physical eyesight nor to any other of the human senses. The latter, by hiding from our gaze, the higher verities (things which we could not bear to behold) are in reality our benefactors, since they prevent us from perceiving that which, if realized without due preparation, would throw us into unutterable consternation. The disciple must be prepared to endure this sight, although he has lost certain supports in the outer world by a realization of the very illusions that encompassed him. It is truly and literally as if his attention were suddenly drawn to a certain danger by which for some time he had been unconsciously threatened. He was not afraid hitherto, but now that he sees his peril, he is overcome by terror, even though the danger has not been rendered any greater by his knowledge thereof.

The forces at work in the world are both destructive and creative. The destiny of manifested beings is birth and death. The Initiate is to behold this march of destiny. The veil, which in the ordinary course of life clouds the spiritual eyes, is to be uplifted, and the man is to see himself as one interwoven with these forces, with this destiny. His own nature contains destructive and creative powers. As undisguisedly as the other objects of his vision are revealed to the eye of the seer, his own soul is bared to his gaze. In the face of this self-knowledge, the disciple must not suffer himself to droop, and in this he will succeed only if he has brought with him an excess of the necessary strength. In order that this may be the case he must learn to maintain inner calm and confidence in the most difficult circumstances; he must nourish within himself a firm faith in the beneficent forces of existence. He must be prepared to find that many motives which have actuated him hitherto will actuate him no longer. He must needs perceive that he has hitherto often thought or acted in a certain manner, because he was still in the toils of ignorance. Reasons which formerly influenced him will now disappear. He has done many things out of personal vanity; he will now perceive how utterly futile all such vanity is in the eyes of the Initiate. He has done much from motives of avarice; he will now be aware of the destructive effect of all avariciousness. He will have to develop entirely new springs for his thought and action, and it is for this that courage and fearlessness are required.

It is especially a matter of cultivating this courage and this fearlessness in the inmost depths of the mental life. The disciple must learn never to despair. He must always be equal to the thought: "I will forget that I have again failed in this matter. I will try once more, as though nothing at all had happened." Thus he will fight his way on to the firm conviction that the universe contains inexhaustible fountains of strength from which he may drink. He must aspire again and again to the

Divine which will uplift and support him, however feeble and impotent the mortal part of his being may prove. He must be capable of pressing on towards the future, undismayed by any experiences of the past. Every teacher of Occultism will carefully ascertain how far the disciple, aspiring to Initiation into the higher mysteries, has advanced on the road of spiritual preparation. If he fulfil these conditions to a certain degree, he is then worthy to hear uttered those Names of things which form the key that unlocks the higher knowledge. For Initiation consists in this very act of learning to know the things of the universe by those Names which they bear in the spirit of their Divine Author. And the mystery of things lies in these Names. Therefore it is that the Initiate speaks another language than that of the uninitiate, for he knows the Names by which things were called into existence.

VI

INITIATION

The highest degree in Occultism, of which it is possible to speak in a book for general readers, is Initiation. One cannot give public information concerning all that lies beyond, though the way to it can always be found by one who has previously pressed forward and penetrated the lower secrets and mysteries.

The knowledge and power which are conferred upon a man through Initiation could not be obtained in any other manner except in some far distant future, after many incarnations, on quite another road and in quite another form. He who is initiated to-day experiences something which he would otherwise have to experience at a much later period and under quite different circumstances.

It is right that a person should learn only so much of the secrets of nature as correspond to his own degree of development, and for this reason alone do obstacles bar his way to complete knowledge and power. People should not be trusted with the use of fire-arms until they have had enough experience to make it certain that they will not use them mischievously or without care. If a person, without the necessary preparation, were initiated to-day, he would still lack those experiences which, in the normal course of his development, would come to him in the future during other incarnations and would then bring with them the corresponding secrets. At the door of Initiation these experiences must, therefore, be supplied in some other way, and in their place the candidate has to undergo the preliminary teaching. These are so-called "trials" which have to be passed. These trials are now being discussed in various books and magazines, but, owing to the very nature of such discussion, it is not surprising that quite false impressions are received concerning them. For those who have not already gone through the periods of Probation and Enlightenment know nothing of these trials, and consequently cannot appropriately describe them.

Certain matters or subjects connected with the higher worlds are produced before the candidate, but he is able to see and hear these only when he can perceive clearly the figures, tones, and colors, for which he has been prepared by the teachings on Probation and Enlightenment.

The first trial consists in obtaining a clearer comprehension of the corporeal attributes of what seem to be lifeless things, then of plants, of animals, of human beings (in the way that the average person possesses them). This does not mean what is commonly called "scientific knowledge"; with that it has no connection, but it has to do with intuition. What usually occurs is that the Initiate discloses to the candidate how the objects of nature and the essence of living things reveal themselves to the spiritual and mental hearing and sight. In a certain way these things then lie revealed—naked—before the beholder. Attributes and qualities which are concealed from physical eyes and ears can then be seen and heard. Heretofore they have been enwrapped as in a veil, and the falling away of this veil for the candidate, occurs at what is called the Process of Purification by Fire. The first trial is therefore known as the "Fire-Trial," which will briefly be explained thus:

For some people the every day ordinary life is a more or less unconscious process of initiation by means of the Fire-Trial. These persons are those who have passed through a wealth of developing experiences, and who find that their self-confidence, courage, and fortitude have been greatly augmented in a normal way—who have learned to bear sorrow and disappointment, from the failure of their undertakings, with greatness of mind, and especially with quiet and unbroken strength. Those who have gone through such experiences are often initiates, without knowing it, and it needs but little to open for them the spiritual hearing and sight—to make them clairvoyant. For it must be noted that a genuine Fire-Trial is not merely intended to satisfy the curiosity of the candidate. He would learn, undoubtedly, many unusual things, of which others, devoid of such experiences, can have no idea; but yet this knowledge is not the end nor aim, but merely the path to the end. The real aim and object is this—that the candidate shall acquire for himself, through this knowledge of the higher worlds, a greater and truer self-confidence, a higher and nobler courage, and a perseverance, an attitude of mind, altogether different from what he could have obtained in the lower world.

After the Fire-Trial a candidate may turn from the school; but because he has gone thus far he will accomplish his ordinary life work, greatly strengthened in all his spiritual and physical relations, and in his next incarnation he will continue to seek further initiation and advancement. In his present life, at all events, he will prove himself a more useful member of society, will be of greater service to humanity than he was before, and in whatever position he may find himself, his firmness, prudence, and favorable influence over his fellows will have greatly increased.

After coming out of the Fire-Trial, if he should wish to continue in the occult school, he then has to be instructed in a certain writing-system which is used by those in the school. Occult teachings are written in this occult writing-system, because what is really occult can neither be perfectly spoken of in words of our ordinary speech, nor set forth in the ordinary ways of writing. Those who have learned much from the Initiates can but partially translate the teachings of Occultism into terms of ordinary speech.

The symbols or signs of the secret script are not arbitrarily invented or imagined, but correspond to powers which are active and efficacious in nature. It is through these symbols or signs that one learns the language of such matters. The candidate immediately sees for himself that these symbols correspond to the figures, tones and colors which he has learned to perceive during the periods of Probation and Enlightenment. He now understands that all which went before was like learning how to spell, and that only now does he begin to read in the higher worlds. All that appeared to him before as separate figures, tones and colors, is now revealed to him as a perfect unity, a coherent harmony, and here, for the first time, he attains a real certainty in observing and following the higher knowledge. Hitherto it was not possible for him to be sure that what he saw had been clearly or correctly perceived. Now, at last, it is possible that a correct understanding between the candidate and the Initiate begin to arise concerning the spheres of the higher worlds. For no matter how close the connection between the two may be, no matter what form their intercourse may take in ordinary life, the Initiate can only communicate to the candidate, on these planes, in the direct form or figures of the secret alphabet.

Through this occult speech the student also learns certain rules of conduct for life, certain duties and obligations, of which, previously, he knew nothing whatever. When he learns to know these rules, he is able to perform actions which have a significance and a meaning such as the actions of another who is not initiated can never possess. The only point of view from which he is now able to look upon things; the only plane from which he can now make manifest his deeds, is that of the higher worlds and the instructions concerning such deeds can only be read, or understood, in the secret script.

Yet it must be clearly understood and emphasized that there are persons who, unconsciously, have the ability or faculty of performing these actions, notwithstanding they have never been in an occult school. Such "helpers of humanity and the world" proceed blessedly and beneficently through life. There are certain fundamental reasons, which cannot be here discussed, why they are in possession of seemingly supernatural gifts. The only difference between these persons and the pupils of an occult school is that the former act unconsciously, while the latter work with a full knowledge, insight, judgment, and understanding of the entire matter in hand. Often the candidate has to win by training that which has been bestowed by a Higher Power upon his fellow, for the good of humanity. One should freely and openly honor these favored ones of God; but he should not, on their account, consider the work of the occult schools unnecessary or superfluous.

Now that the student has learned the "Mystery language," there awaits him yet another trial. By this he must prove whether he can move with freedom and certainty in the higher worlds. In ordinary life a man will be impelled to actions by outward motives and conditions. He works at this or that because certain duties are imposed upon him by outward circumstances. It need hardly be mentioned that the occult student must in no way neglect any of the duties connected with his ordinary life because he is a student in an occult school and in the higher worlds. None of his duties there can constrain him to treat with inattention or carelessness any one of his duties in the lower world. The father will remain just as good a father to his family, the mother just as good a mother; and neither the officer nor the soldier, nor anyone else, will be detained from their necessary duties because they are students in Occultism. On the contrary, all the qualities which make capable men are increased to a degree of which the uninitiated can form no idea. That this may not always appear to be the case is due merely to the fact that they have not always the ability to correctly judge or criticize the Initiate. The deeds of the latter are not always entirely intelligible to the former. But, as we have said before, this only happens in certain cases.

For him who has arrived at the so-called "Steps of Initiation," there are new duties to be performed to which no outer stimulus is given. He will be moved to do these things by no external pressure, but by those rules of conduct which have been communicated to him in the mystery-language. In this second trial he must prove that, led by such rules of conduct, he can act from inner promptings just as firmly as an officer performs his obligatory duties. For this purpose the teacher will set before the pupil certain definite tasks. The latter now has to perform some deed in consequence of observations made from the total of what he learned during Probation and Enlightenment. He has to find the way to what he is now to perform, by means of the mystery-language, which by this time is familiar to him. If he discerns his duty and executes it correctly, he has endured the trial, and he recognizes the success, which attends the fulfilment of the task, by the changed manner with which the spiritual eyes and ears now apprehend the figures, tones and colors. The occult teacher tells him distinctly how these must appear after the consummation of the trial, and the candidate must know how he can effect this change. This trial is known as the "Water-Trial," because, in consequence of its performance taking place on the higher planes, that support, which would otherwise have been received from outward conditions, is now taken away. One's movements are like those which are made in water by someone learning to swim, and his feelings are those of one having no support except his own efforts. This practice must be often repeated until the candidate attains absolute poise and assurance.

These trials are also dependent upon a quality which is produced by his experiences in the higher worlds. The candidate cultivates this quality to an extent which he could not possibly reach in so short a time while developing in the ordinary way, but could attain only after many incarnations. In order to bring about the change here mentioned, the following condition is necessary: The candidate must be guided altogether by what has been proven to him by the cultivation of his higher faculties, by the results of his reading in the secret symbols.

Should he, during these experiences, attempt to introduce any of his own opinions or desires, or should he diverge for one moment from the laws and rules which he has proved to be right, something quite other than that which is expected will occur. In such cases the candidate loses sight of the goal for which these matters are undertaken, and the result is confusion. He has, therefore, manifold opportunities, during these trials, for the development of self-control, and this, indeed, is the principal quality needed. These trials are, therefore, much more easily endured by those who, before initiation, have gone through a life which has enabled them to acquire command of themselves. Those who have developed the characteristic of following their higher principles and ideals without thought of personal honor or desire, who always discern the duty to be fulfilled, even though the inclinations and sympathies are too often ready to lead them another way, are already unconscious initiates in the midst of every day life. They need but little to enable them to succeed in the prescribed trials. Indeed, one may say that a certain measure of initiation, thus unconsciously acquired in life, will be absolutely necessary before entering upon the second trial. For even as many who during youth have not learned to write or spell, find much difficulty in learning to do so in later years, so is it also difficult to develop, merely from a knowledge of the higher worlds, the necessary degree of self-control, if one has not already acquired a certain measure of it in the course of ordinary life.

The things of the physical world do not alter by merely desiring them to do so, but in the higher worlds our wishes, inclinations and desires are causes that produce effects. If we wish to bring about particular changes in these worlds, we must hold ourselves in absolute control, we must follow the right principle, must entirely subdue the personal will.

There is an attribute which at this stage of initiation has to be especially considered,—a really healthy and sure faculty of judgment. Attention must be directed to the education of this faculty during all the previous stages, and in the course of them it must be proven whether the candidate has developed this quality sufficiently to make him fit to tread the path of true knowledge, for, further progress is now possible only if he is able to distinguish illusion, superstition, unsubstantial fancies, and all manner of such things, from the true realities. At first, this is much more difficult to accomplish upon the higher stages of existence than upon the lower. Every prejudice, every cherished opinion regarding these matters, in whatever connection, must be banished. Truth alone must guide. There must be perfect readiness to surrender at once any existing opinion, idea, or inclination, when the logical idea demands it. Absolute certainty in the higher worlds can be obtained only when one does not obtrude his own opinions.

People whose mode of thought inclines them to phantasy, prejudice and so forth, can make no progress on the occult way. Yet be not dismayed—there is, in truth, a glorious treasure that the persistent occult student shall attain. All doubt as to the higher worlds will be taken away from him. In all their law they will reveal themselves to his gaze, but so long as he is blindfolded he cannot see these heights and compensations. It is, indeed, unfortunate for him if illusions and fallacies ran away with his intellect and reason. Dreamers and people inclined to phantasies, are as unfit for the occult path as are superstitious people; for in dreams, illusions and superstitions lurk the most dangerous enemies on the road to knowledge. Because the candidate has already seen upon the portals that opened to him the first trial, the words, "Without a normal common-sense all your efforts are in vain;" and upon the gateway, which leads to the second trial, "All prejudices must fall away," it is not necessary to think that the capacity for inspiration and enthusiasm, and all the poetry of life, is lost to the student of Occultism.

If he be now sufficiently advanced, a third trial awaits the candidate. No aim, no boundary lines, are here set for him. All is left entirely in his own hands. He finds himself in a condition where nothing external impels or induces him to act. He must find the way of his own accord and from within himself. Conditions or people who might have stimulated him to action are no longer there. Nothing and nobody but he himself alone can give the strength which he now needs. If he should not find this strength within he will very soon be standing where he was before; but it should be stated that very few of those who have endured the previous trials will fail at this point in finding the necessary strength. If they have come so far they will endure at this point also. The only thing necessary is the ability to make a resolution quickly. For here, in the truest meaning of the phrase, one must find oneself. In all matters one must instantly resolve to hear the suggestions, the inspirations of the spirit. One has no time for doubt or delay. Every moment of hesitation would add to the proof that one was not yet ready. All that hinders one from hearing the voice of the spirit must be boldly conquered. It is entirely a matter of proving one's presence of mind, and it is this attribute to which attention must be paid during all the foregoing stages of development. All temptations to act, or even to think, which hitherto assailed a man, must here cease; but in order that he may not slip into inaction, he must not lose his hold upon himself. For only in himself can he find that one sure centre-point on which he can depend. No one should feel an antipathy to this principle of self-rejection. For him who has endured the trials already described, it indicates the most perfect felicity.

In this, as in the other stages before mentioned, every day life itself can, for many people, be an occult school. Those who have reached the point of being able to act without delay or personal consideration and can make prompt resolutions when suddenly confronted with some task or problem demanding immediate action, have, indeed, undergone their occult schooling in daily life. The situation which one wishes to suggest is one in which a successful action is impossible unless the person concerned grasps the whole matter and acts at once. He is quick to act when misfortune is in sight, while a moment's hesitation might lead to a catastrophe; and he who possesses the qualities which can be developed into a permanent attribute of such a kind, has already evolved, unknown to himself, the degree of ripeness necessary for the third trial. For, as already remarked, at this stage all depends upon the development of presence of mind.

In the occult schools this trial is known as the "Air-Trial," because while undergoing it, the candidate cannot support himself either upon the firm ground, or any external cause, or that which he has learned in Probation and Enlightenment—from the figures and tones and colors, but solely upon himself.

If the occult student has endured these trials, he is then permitted to enter "the Temple of the Higher Wisdom." All that can be said further upon this subject can be given out only in the smallest hints and suggestions. The responsibility of the next step has so often been illy expressed by words, that many say the pupil has here to take an "oath," promising to betray nothing that comes from the teacher. However, these expressions, "oath" and "betrayal," are in no way appropriate, and are misleading.

It is no oath, in the ordinary sense of the word, but is rather an experience that comes at this stage. Here the candidate appreciates the true value of the occult teachers, and their place in the service of humanity. At last he begins to understand the world correctly. It is not so much a matter of "withholding" the higher truths already learned, but much more of upholding them in the right way and with the necessary tact. That concerning which one learns to "keep silence" is something quite different. One gains possession of this fine attribute in regard to many things of which one had previously spoken, and especially in regard to the manner in which one has spoken of them. Yet he would be a poor Initiate who did not place all his mystical experiences, as adequately and as far-reachingly as possible, at the service of humanity. The sole obstacle in such matters is the misunderstanding of the person who receives the communication. Above all, the higher or occult secrets are not allowed to be spoken of promiscuously, but no one who has passed the steps of development above described, is it actually forbidden to speak of these matters. No one is asked for a negative oath, but everything is entrusted to the judgment, integrity and sense of responsibility of the candidate for Initiation. What one really learns is to find out, within oneself, what should be done under all circumstances, and the "oath" means nothing more than this, that one is found qualified to be entrusted with matters of such importance.

If the candidate is found fit, he is then given what is called, symbolically, "the draught of forgetfulness." This means that he will be initiated into the secret knowledge enabling him to act without being continually disturbed by the lower memory. This is absolutely necessary for the Initiate, for he must possess full faith in the immediate present. He must be able to destroy that veil of memory which extends itself round humanity more and more thickly with every moment of life.

If one judges things which happen to-day, by the experiences of yesterday, he is subjected to a multitude of errors. Of course, it is not intended that the reader should renounce all the experience acquired in life. He ought always to keep it in mind as firmly as possible. But, as an Initiate, one should acquire the ability to judge every fresh experience irrespective of oneself, unclouded by all bygone experiences. One must be prepared, at every moment, that a new thing or being shall bring to one a new revelation. If one judges the new by the standard of the old, he necessarily falls into error. The memory of past experiences is very useful, however, for it makes one better able to perceive the new. If one had not gone through a certain experience, he probably would not have seen the attributes of this or that being or thing; but having had such experiences he ought to be enabled to discern the new, without judging it by the old. In this way the Initiate obtains certain definite qualities, and by means of these many things are revealed to him, while they remain concealed from the uninitiated.

The second draught which is given to the Initiate is the "draught of remembrance." By receiving this he becomes capable of keeping the higher secrets ever present in the soul. Ordinary memory would not be sufficient to ensure this; he must be absolutely at one with the higher truths. He must not merely know them, but be able, as a matter of course, to manifest and administer them in living actions, even as an ordinary man eats and drinks. They must become one's practice, one's inclinations, one's habits. It must be unnecessary to recall them to mind (in the usual sense of the term); they must become a part of oneself and express themselves through one's very being; they must flow through one, just as the life-currents run through one's bodily organism. So must we make ourselves as perfect in a spiritual sense as nature has made us in a physical.

VII

THE HIGHER EDUCATION OF THE SOUL

If a man carries out the culture of his thoughts and feelings and emotions in the way already described in the chapters on Probation, Enlightenment, and Initiation, he then effects a change in his soul such as Nature has effected in his body. Before this training, soul and spirit are undifferentiated masses. In such a state the clairvoyant will perceive them as interlacing clouds, rotating spirally, and having usually a dull glimmer of reddish or reddish-brown color, or, perhaps, of reddish-yellow; but after this growth they begin to assume a brilliant yellowish-green or yellow-blue hue, and become of a regular structure. A man attains such regularity of structure, and at the same time the higher knowledge, when he brings into the realm of his thoughts, feelings and emotions, an order, such as Nature has brought into his bodily organs, by means of which he can see, hear, digest, breathe, speak and so forth. Gradually the student learns, as it were, to breathe, to see with the soul, and to speak and hear with the spirit.

In the following pages a few of the practical points pertaining to the higher education of the soul and spirit will be more fully treated. They are such as may be practically attained by anyone without additional instruction, and by means of which a further step in occult science may be taken.

A particular kind of discipline must be patiently attempted such as to avoid every emotion of impatience, for it produces a paralyzing, yea, even a deadening, effect on the higher faculties within us. One must not expect immeasurable glimpses of the higher worlds to open out before one from day to day, for assuredly, as a rule, this does not occur. Contentment with the smallest progress, repose and tranquility must more and more possess the soul. It is conceivable, of course, that the learner may impatiently expect results, but he will attain nothing so long as he fails to master this impatience. Nor is it of any use to struggle against this impatience in the ordinary way, for then it will only become stronger than ever. It is thus that men deceive themselves, for in such a case it embeds itself all the more firmly in the depths of the soul. It is only by repeatedly surrendering oneself to a single definite thought, and by making it absolutely one's own, that anything is really attained. One should think: "I must certainly do everything possible for the culture of soul and spirit, but I will work tranquilly until, by higher powers, I shall be found worthy of definite illumination." When this thought has become so powerful in a man that it is an actual trait in his character, he is treading the right path. This trait will then express itself even in external affairs. The gaze of the eye becomes tranquil; the movements of the body become sure; the resolutions defined; and all that we call nervous susceptibility gradually disappears. Rules that seem trifling and insignificant must be taken into account. For example, suppose that someone affronts us. Before we receive this occult education, we would have directed our resentment against the wrong-doer; there would have been an uprush of anger within us. But in such a case the occult student will think to himself: "An affront of this kind can make no difference to my worth," and whatever must be done to meet the affront, he accomplishes with calm and composure, not with passion. To him it is not a matter of how an affront is to be borne, but without hesitation he is led to ignore or punish the affront to his own person in exactly the same way as if it had been offered to another, in which case one has the right to resent or disregard it. It must always be remembered, however, that the occult training is perfected not by coarse external processes, but by subtle, silent alterations in the life of thought and emotion.

Patience has an attractive, while impatience has a repellent, effect on the treasures of the higher knowledge. In the higher regions of being, nothing can be attained by haste and restlessness. Desire and longing for immediate results must be silenced, for these are qualities of the soul before which all higher knowledge recedes. However precious this knowledge may be accounted, one must not desire to anticipate the time of its coming. And, furthermore, he who wishes to have it for his own sake alone will never attain it. It is absolutely demanded that one should be true to himself in his innermost soul. One must not there be deceived by anything; he must encounter, face to face and with absolute truthfulness, his own faults, failings, and unfitness. The moment you try to excuse to yourself any one of your weaknesses, you place an obstacle in the way which leads upward. There is one way only by which to get rid of such obstacles. Our faults and weaknesses can be removed only by self-illumination, and that is by correctly understanding them. All that is needed lies latent in the human soul and can be evoked. A man immediately improves his understanding and his reason when in repose he makes it clear to himself why he is weak in any respect. Self-knowledge of this kind is naturally difficult, for the temptation to deceive oneself is immeasurably great. He who is accustomed to be truthful with himself has opened the portals into a deeper insight.

All curiosity must fall away from the student. He must wean himself as much as possible from inquiries into matters of which he wishes to know only for the gratification of his personal thirst for superficial information. He must ask himself only what things will assist him in the perfection of his innermost being for the service of the general evolution. Nevertheless, his delight in knowledge and his devotion to it must in no degree become relaxed. He must listen devoutly to all that contributes to such an end, and should seek every opportunity of doing so.

For this interior culture it is especially necessary that the desire-life should be carefully educated. One must not become wholly destitute of desire, for if we are to accomplish something it is necessary that we should desire it, and a desire will always be fulfilled if a certain special force is behind it. This particular force results from a right knowledge: "Do not desire at all until you know the true conditions of any sphere." That is one of the golden rules for the occult student. The wise man first ascertains the laws of the world, and then his desires become powers which realize themselves. Let us consider an example in which the effect is evident. There are certainly many who would like to learn from their own intuition something about their life before birth. Such a desire is altogether aimless, and leads to no result so long as the person in question has not acquired a knowledge of the laws that govern the nature of the Eternal, and a knowledge of them in their subtlest and most intimate character.

But if he has actually acquired this knowledge and then wishes to pass onward, he is able to do so by his elevated and purified desire.

Moreover, it is of no use to say to oneself: "Yes, I will forthwith examine my previous life, and study with that aim in view." One must rather be ready to abandon such desire, to eliminate it altogether, and first of all, learn, without consideration of this aim. One should cultivate devotion to knowledge without regard to desires. It is only then that one enters into possession of the desire which we are considering, in a way that leads to its own fulfilment.

From one's anger or vexation arises an adverse condition in the spiritual world, so that those forces which would open the eyes of the soul are turned away. For example, if someone should annoy me, he sends forth a current into the world of the soul. So long as I allow myself to be annoyed, I cannot see this current. My own annoyance clouds it. But from this it must not be supposed that when I no longer feel annoyed I will see the astral vision. To see an astral vision it is indispensable that the eye of the soul should already be developed; but the capacity for sight of this kind is latent in everyone. And again it is true that during the development, so long as one can be annoyed the sight remains inactive; nor does it present itself immediately, when one has overcome to a small extent this feeling of annoyance. One must continually persevere in the struggle with such a feeling, and patiently make progress: then, some day, he will find that this eye of the soul has become fully developed. Of course annoyance is not the only quality with which we have to struggle before attaining this end. Many people grow impatient or sceptical, because they have for years cultivated certain qualities of the soul and yet clairvoyance has not ensued. They have developed only a few qualities and have allowed others to run wild. The gift of clairvoyance first manifests itself when all those qualities which do not permit the development of the latent faculties are suppressed. Undoubtedly the beginnings of such hearing and seeing may appear at an earlier period, but these are only young and tender shoots which are subject to all possible error, and which, if they be not carefully fostered, may quickly die.

The qualities which have to be combated, in addition to anger and vexation, are such as ambition, timidity, curiosity, superstition, conceit, the disease of prejudice, idle love of gossip, and the making of distinctions in regard to human beings according to the merely outward marks of rank, sex, race, and so forth. In our time it is difficult for people to comprehend that the combating of such qualities can have any connection with an increase of capacity for knowledge. But every devotee of Occultism is aware that much more depends upon such matters than upon the expansion of the intellect or the employment of artificial practices. It is particularly easy for a misunderstanding of this point to arise, inasmuch as many believe that one should cultivate foolhardiness because one must be fearless, and that one should ignore altogether the differences in men because one has to combat the prejudices of race, rank, and so forth. Rather should one first learn to appreciate these differences correctly, then one is no longer entangled in prejudice. Even in the usual sense it is true that a fear of any phenomenon hinders one from estimating it rightly; that a race-prejudice prevents one from looking into a man's soul. The student of Occultism must bring his common-sense to perfection in all its exactitude and subtlety.

Even everything that a man says without having clearly thought it out will place an obstacle in the path of his occult education. At the same time we must here consider one point which can only be elucidated by giving an example. Thus, if anyone should say something to which another must reply, the one replying should be careful to consider the intention, the feelings, even the prejudices of this other person, rather than what he has to say at the moment on the subject under discussion. In other words, the student must apply himself keenly to the cultivation of a certain fine tact. He must learn to judge how much it may mean to this other person if his opinion be opposed. It must not be imagined for a moment that he ought for this reason, to withhold his own opinion. One must give to the questioner as careful a hearing as possible, and from what one has heard, formulate one's own reply. In such cases there is a certain thought which will constantly recur to the student, and he is treading the true path if this thought becomes so vital within him that it grows into a trait of his character. The thought is as follows: "It matters little whether my view be different from his, the vital point is whether he will discover the right view for himself if I am able to contribute something towards it." By thoughts of such a kind, the mode of action and the character of the student will become permeated with gentleness, one of the most essential qualities for the reception of occult teaching. Harshness obscures that internal image which ought to be evoked by the eye of the soul, while by gentleness many obstacles are cleared from the way, and the inner organs opened.

Along with this gentleness another trait will presently be developed in the soul. He will make a quiet estimate of all the subtleties in the soul-life around him, without considering the emotions of his own soul. And if this condition has been attained, the soul-emotions in the environment of others will have such an effect on him that the soul within him grows, and, growing, becomes organized, as a plant expands in the sunlight. Gentleness, quiet reserve, and true patience, open the soul to the world of souls, and the spirit to the realm of spirits. Persevere in repose and retirement; close the senses to that which they brought you before you began your training; bring into utter stillness all those thoughts which, in accordance with your previous habits, were tossed up and down within you; become quite still and silent within, wait in patience, and then the tranquil higher worlds will begin to develop the sight of your soul and the hearing of your spirit. Do not suppose that you will immediately see and hear in the worlds of soul and spirit, for all that you are doing does but help the development of your higher senses, and you will not be able to see with the soul and to hear with the spirit before you have to some degree acquired those senses. When you have persevered for a time in repose and retirement, then go about your daily affairs, having first impressed upon your mind the thought: "Some day, when I am ready, I shall attain what I am to attain." Finally: "Make no attempt whatever to attract any of these higher powers to yourself by an effort of the will." These are instructions which every occult student receives from his teacher at the entrance of the way. If he observes them, he then improves himself; and if he does not observe them, all his labor is in vain; but they are difficult of achievement for him only who has not patience and perseverance. No other obstacles exist save those which one places for oneself, and these may be avoided by anyone if he really wills it. It is necessary to continually insist upon this point, because many people form an altogether wrong conception of the difficulty that lies in the path of Occultism. In a certain sense, it is easier to accomplish the earlier steps of the occult way, than it is for one who has received no instruction, to get rid of the difficulties of one's every-day life. In addition to this, it must be understood that only such things are here imparted as are attended by no danger to the health of soul or body. There are certain other ways which lead more quickly to the goal, but it is not well to treat of them publicly, because they may sometimes have certain effects on a man which would necessitate the immediate intervention of an experienced teacher, and in any case would require his continual supervision. Now, as something about these quicker ways frequently forces itself into publicity, it becomes necessary to give express warning against entering upon them without personal guidance. For reasons which only the initiated can understand, it will never be possible to give public instruction concerning these other ways in their true form, and the fragments which here and there make their appearance can never lead to anything profitable, but may easily result in the undermining of health, fortune and peace of mind. He who does not wish to put himself in the power of certain dark forces, of whose nature and origin he may know nothing, had far better avoid meddling in such matters.

Something may here be added concerning the environment in which the practices of occult instruction ought to be undertaken. This is of great importance, although for almost every man the case is different. He who practices in an environment which is only filled with selfish interests, as for example, the modern struggle for existence, ought to be sure that these interests are without influence upon the development of his spiritual organs. It is true that the inner laws of these organs are so powerful that this influence cannot be fatally injurious. Just as a lily, however inappropriate the environment in which it may be placed, can never become a thistle, so the eye of the soul can never grow to anything but its destined end, even though it be subjected to all the modern reverse influences. But it is well if, under all circumstances, the student should now and then seek for his environment the quietude, the inner dignity, the sweetness of Nature herself. Especially fortunate are the conditions of him who is able to pursue his occult studies in the green world of plants, or among the sunny mountains or the delightful interplay of simple things. This develops the inner organs in a degree of harmony which is difficult to obtain amid the noise and commercialism of a modern city. He also is more favorably situated than the mere townsman, who, during his childhood at least, was able to breathe the perfume of the pines, to gaze on the snowy peaks, or observe the silent activity of woodland creatures and insects. Yet no one who is obliged to live in a city should fail to give his evolving soul and spirit the nurture that comes from the inspired utterances of the mighty teachers of man. He who cannot every springtime follow day by day the unfolding of the greenwood, ought in its place to draw into his heart the sublime doctrines of the Bhagavad Gîtâ, or of St. John's Gospel, or of Thomas à Kempis. There are various paths to the summit of insight, but a right selection is invaluable.

The adept in Occultism could, indeed, say much concerning these paths—much that might seem strange to an uninitiated hearer. For example, suppose that someone has advanced far along the occult path, and wholly unaware of his nearness, may be standing at the entrance to the sight of the soul and the hearing of the spirit, and then he has the good fortune to pass peacefully into its very presence, and a bandage falls away from the eyes of his soul. Suddenly he can see—his vision is attained! Another, it may be, has advanced so far that this bandage needs only to be loosened, and by some stroke of destiny this occurs. For another one this very stroke might actually have the effect of paralyzing his powers and undermining his energy, but for the occult student it becomes the occasion of his enlightenment. Perhaps a third has patiently persevered for years, and without any marked result. Suddenly, while tranquilly seated in his quiet chamber, light envelops him, the walls become transparent, they vanish away, and a new world expands before his opened eyes, or is audible to his awakened spirit.

VIII

THE CONDITIONS OF DISCIPLESHIP

The conditions of entrance into an occult school are not of a nature to be formulated in an arbitrary way by anyone. They are the natural outcome of occult knowledge. Just as a man will never become a painter if he does not choose to handle a paintbrush, so can no one receive occult training if he is unwilling to fulfil the claims which are put forward by the occult teacher. In fact, the teacher can give nothing but advice, and it is as such that everything he states ought to be considered. He has already trodden the probationary path which leads to the knowledge of higher worlds. From experience he knows what is necessary, and it all depends on the free will of each particular person whether he chooses to follow the same path or not. If anyone, without intending to satisfy the conditions, should demand occult training from a teacher, such a demand would be equivalent to saying: "Teach me to paint, but do not ask me to handle a brush." The occult teacher never goes a step further, unless it be in accord with the free will of the recipient. It must be emphasized that a general wish for higher knowledge is not sufficient, yet many will probably have but such a weak desire. For him who has merely this vague idea, and is not prepared to accept the special conditions of the occult teacher, the latter, for the present, can do nothing. This ought to be kept in mind by those who complain that occult teachers do not "meet them half way." He who cannot, or will not, fulfil the severe conditions necessary, must for the time abandon occult training. It is true that the conditions are, indeed, hard, and yet they are not severe since their fulfilment not only ought to be, but must be, an altogether voluntary deed.

To him who does not remember this it is easy for the claims of the occult teacher to seem a coercion of the soul or the conscience; for the training here mentioned is founded on a development of the inner life, and it is the work of the teacher to give advice concerning it. And yet, if something be demanded as the result of free choice, it cannot be considered as a fetter. If anyone says to the teacher: "Give me your secrets, but leave me my customary feelings and thoughts," he is then making an impossible demand. Such an one desires no more than to satisfy his curiosity and thirst for sensations, so that by one who takes an attitude like this, occult knowledge can never be obtained.

Let us now consider in their right order the conditions of discipleship. It should be emphasized that the complete fulfilment of any one of these conditions is by no means demanded, but only the effort to gain such fulfilment. No one can at first reach these high ideals, but the path which leads to their fulfilment may be entered by everyone. It is the will that matters, the attitude taken when entering the path.

1. The first condition is the directing of the attention to the advancement of bodily and spiritual health. Of course, discipleship does not in the first place depend on the health of a man, but everyone can endeavor to improve in this respect, and only from a healthy man may proceed a healthy perception. No occult teacher would refuse a man who is not healthy, but it is demanded that the pupils should have the desire for a healthy

life. In this respect he must attain the greatest possible independence. The good counsels of others, which, though generally unsought, are received by everybody, are as a rule superfluous. Each must endeavor to take care of himself. From the physical aspect it will be more a matter of warding off harmful influences than of anything else. For in carrying out one's duty one has often to do things which are disadvantageous to health. One must learn how, at the right moment, to place duty higher than the care of health; but with a little good-will, what is there that cannot be omitted? Duty must in many cases be accounted higher than health, indeed, if need be, higher than life itself, but the disciple must never put pleasure as high as either one of these. Pleasure for him can be only a means to health and life, and in respect to this it is absolutely necessary that we should be quite honest and truthful with ourselves. It is of no avail to lead an ascetic life so long as it is born of motives like those that give rise to other enjoyments. There are people who find satisfaction in asceticism, as do others in wine-bibbling, but they must not imagine that asceticism of this kind will assist them to attain the higher knowledge. Many ascribe to their unfavorable circumstances everything which apparently prevents them from making progress in this direction. They say that with their conditions of life they cannot develop themselves to any great extent. For other reasons it may be desirable for many to change their conditions of life, but no one need do so for the purpose of occult training. For this it is only necessary that one should do for one's health so much as one finds possible in the position one holds. Every kind of work may serve the whole of humanity, and it is a surer sign of greatness in the human soul to perceive clearly how necessary for the whole is a petty—

perhaps even an unlovely—employment than to think: "This work is not good enough for me: I am destined for something else."

It is especially important for the disciple to strive after complete spiritual health. In any case, an unhealthy emotional or thought-life leads one away from the path of higher knowledge. The foundations here consist of clear, calm thinking, reliable conceptions, and stable feelings. Nothing should be more alien to the disciple than an inclination toward a whimsical, excitable life, toward nervousness, intoxication, and fanaticism. He should acquire a healthy outlook on all circumstances of life; he should go through life steadily and should let things act on him and speak to him in all tranquillity. Wherever it is possible he should endeavor to do justice to life. Everything in his tastes and criticisms which is one-sided or extravagant ought to be avoided. If this be not so, the disciple will strand himself in a world of his own imagination, instead of attaining the higher worlds, and in place of truth his own favorite opinions will assert themselves. It is better for the disciple to be "matter-of-fact" than overwrought and fanciful.

2. The second condition is that one should feel oneself as a link in the general life. Much is included in the fulfilment of this condition, but each can only fulfil it after his own manner. If I am a school teacher and my pupil does not answer what is desired of him, I must first direct my feeling not against the pupil but to myself. I ought to feel myself so much at one with my pupil that I ask myself: "May not that in the pupil which does not satisfy my demand be perhaps the result of my own faults?" or if perchance it be his unconscious, or even vicious

error, as teacher, instead of directing my feelings against him, I shall rather cogitate on the way in which I myself ought to behave, or in kindness show him what is right, so that he may in the future be better able to satisfy my demands. From such a manner of thinking there will come gradually a change over the whole mental attitude. This holds good for the smallest as well as for the greatest. From this point of view I look on a criminal, for instance, altogether differently from the way I should have looked upon him of old. I suspend my judgment and think to myself: "I am only a man as he is. Perhaps the education which, owing to favorable circumstances, has been mine, and nothing else, has saved me from a similar fate." I may even come to the conclusion that if the teachers who took pains with me had done the same for him, this brother of mine would have been quite different. I shall reflect on the fact that something which has been withheld from him has been given to me, and that I may, perhaps, owe my goodness to the fact that he has been thus deprived of it. And then will it no longer be difficult to grasp the conception that I am a link in the whole of humanity, and that consequently I, too, in part, bear the responsibility for everything that happens. By this it is not implied that such a thought should be translated immediately into external action. It should be quietly cultivated in the soul. It will then express itself gradually in the outward behavior of a person, and in such matters each can begin only by reforming himself. It were futile, from such a standpoint, to make general claims on all humanity. It is easy to form an idea of what men ought to be, but the disciple works, not on the surface, but in the depths. And, therefore, it would be wrong if one should endeavor to bring these demands of the occult teacher into relation with any external or political claims.

As a rule, political agitators know well what can be demanded of other people, but they say little of demands on themselves.

3. Now with these demands on ourselves the third condition for occult training is intimately connected. The student must be able to realize the idea that his thoughts and feelings are as important for the world as his deeds. It must be recognized that it is as pernicious to hate a fellow-being as to strike him. One can then discern also that by perfecting oneself one accomplishes something not only for oneself but for the whole world. The world profits by pure thoughts and feelings as much as by one's good behavior, and so long as one cannot believe in this world-wide importance of the inner Self, one is not fit for discipleship. One is permeated with a true conception of the soul's importance, only when one works at this inner Self as if it were at least as important as all external things. It must be admitted that one's feelings produce an effect as much as the action of the hand.

4. In so saying we have already mentioned the fourth condition: the idea that the real being of man does not lie in the exterior but in the interior. He who regards himself as merely a product of the outer world, a result of the physical world, cannot succeed in this occult training. But he who is able to realize this conception is then also able to distinguish between inner duty and external success. He learns to recognize that the one cannot at once be measured by the other. The student must learn for himself the right position between what is demanded by his external conditions and what he recognizes to be the right conduct for himself. He ought not to force upon his environment anything for which it can have no appreciation, but at the same time he

must be altogether free from the desire to do merely what can be appreciated by those around him. In his own sincere and wisdom-seeking soul, and only there, must he look for the recognition of his truths. But from his environment he must learn as much as he possibly can, so that he may discern what those around him need, and what is of use to them. In this way he will develop within himself what is known in Occultism as the "spiritual balance." On one side of the scales there lies a heart open for the needs of the outward world, and on the other lies an inner fortitude and an unfaltering endurance.

5. And here, again, we have hinted at the fifth condition: firmness in the carrying out of any resolution when once it has been made. Nothing should induce the disciple to deviate from any such resolution once it is formed, save only the perception that he has made a mistake. Every resolution is a force, and even if such a force does not produce immediate effect on the point at which it was directed, nevertheless it works in its own way. Success is of great importance only when an action arises from desire, but all actions which are rooted in desire are worthless in relation to the higher worlds. There the love expended on an action is alone of importance. In this love, all that impels the student to perform an action ought to be implanted. Thus he will never grow weary of again and again carrying out in action some resolution, even though he has repeatedly failed. And in this way he arrives at the condition in which he does not first count on the external effect of his actions, but is contented with the doing of them. He will learn to sacrifice for the world his actions, nay, more, his whole being, without caring at all how his sacrifice may be received. He who wishes to become a disciple must declare himself ready for such a sacrifice, such an offering.

6. A sixth condition is the development of a sense of gratitude with regard to everything which relates to Man. One must realize that one's existence is, as it were, a gift from the entire universe. Only consider all that is needed in order that each of us may receive and maintain his existence! Consider what we owe to Nature and to others than ourselves! Those who desire an occult training must be inclined toward thoughts like these, for he who cannot enter into such thoughts will be incapable of developing within himself that all-inclusive love which it is necessary to possess before one can attain to higher knowledge. That which we do not love cannot manifest itself to us. And every manifestation must fill us with gratitude, or we ourselves are not the richer for it.

7. All the conditions here set forth must be united in a seventh: to regard life continually in the manner demanded by these conditions. The student thus makes it possible to give to his life the stamp of uniformity. All his many modes of expression will, in this way, be brought into harmony, and cease to contradict each other. And thus he will prepare himself for the peace which he must attain during the preliminary steps of his training.

If a person intend, earnestly and sincerely, to fulfil the conditions mentioned above, he may then address himself to a teacher of Occultism. The latter will then be found ready to give the first words of counsel. Any external formality will consist of giving to these conditions a complete expression, a knowledge of which can only be imparted orally to each individual candidate. Since everything interior must manifest itself in an exterior way, they teach a very important lesson. Even as a picture cannot be said to be here, when it exists only in the brain of the painter, so, too, there cannot be an occult training without an external expression.

External forms are regarded as worthless by those only who do not know that the internal must find expression in the external. It is true that it is the spirit and not the form that really matters; but just as the form is void without the spirit, so would the spirit remain inactive as long as it could not create a form.

The stipulated conditions are so designed that they may render the disciple strong enough to fulfil the further demands which the teacher must make. If he be faulty in the fulfilment of these conditions, then before each new demand he will stand hesitating. Without this fulfilment he will be lacking in that faith in man which it is necessary for him to possess; for on faith in man and a genuine love for man, all striving after truth must be founded. And the love of man must be slowly widened out into a love for all living creatures, nay, indeed, for all existence. He who fails to fulfil the conditions here given will not possess a perfect love for all up-building, for all creation, nor a tendency to abstain from all destruction and annihilation as such. The disciple must so train himself that, not in deeds only, but also in words, thoughts and feelings, he will never destroy anything for the sake of destruction. He must find his pleasure in the growing and creating aspect of things, and is only justified in assisting the apparent destruction of anything when, by such readjustment, he is able to promote a greater life. Let it not be thought that, in so saying, it is implied that the disciple may allow the triumph of evil, but rather that he must endeavor to find, even in the bad, those aspects through which he may change it into good. He will see more and more clearly that the best way to combat imperfection and evil is by the creation of the perfect and the good. The student knows that nothing can come from nothing, but also that the imperfect may be changed into the perfect. He who develops in himself the tendency to create, will soon find the capacity for facing the evil.

He who enters an occult school must be quite sure that his intention is to construct and not to destroy. The student ought, therefore, to bring with him the will for sincere and devoted work, and to this end he ought to be capable of great devotion, for one should be anxious to learn what one does not yet know; he should look reverently on that which discloses itself. Work and devotion,—these are the fundamental attributes which must be claimed from the disciple. Some will have to discover that they do not make real progress in the school, even if in their own opinion they are unceasingly active; they have not grasped in the right manner the meaning of work and meditation. That kind of learning which is undertaken without meditation will advance the student least, and the work which is done for selfish returns will be the least successful. In the love of work, the love to do better work; yes, the love to do perfect work, is the quality which unfolds occult power; and in qualifying for better things one need give little heed for greater returns. If he who is learning seeks for wholesome thoughts and sound judgment, he need not spoil his devotion with doubts and suspicions.

The fact that one does not oppose some communication which has been made, but gives to it due attention and even sympathy, does not imply a lack of independent judgment. Those who have arrived at a somewhat advanced stage of knowledge are aware that they owe everything to a quiet attention and assimilation, and not to a stubborn personal judgment. One should always remember that he does not need to learn what he is already able to understand. Therefore, if one desires only to judge, he is apt to cease learning. What is of importance in an occult school, however, is study: one ought to desire, with heart and soul, to be a student: if one cannot understand something it is far better not to judge, lest one wrongly condemn; far wiser to wait for a true understanding. The higher one climbs up the ladder of knowledge, the more he requires this faculty of calm and devotional listening. All perception of truths, all life and activity in the world of spirit, become in these higher regions delicate and subtle in comparison with the activities of the ordinary mind, and of life in the physical world. The more the sphere of a man's activity widens out before him, the more transcendent is the nature of the task to be accomplished by him. It is for this reason that, although there is in reality only one possible fact regarding the higher truths, men come to look at them from such different points of view. It is possible to arrive at this one true standpoint if, through work and devotion, one has so risen that he can really behold the truth. Only he who judges in accordance with preconceived ideas and habitual ways of thought, rather than from sufficient preparation, can arrive at any opinion which differs from the true one. Just as there is only one correct opinion concerning a mathematical problem, so also with regard to things of the higher worlds; but before one can arrive at this knowledge he must first prepare himself. Truth and the higher life do, indeed, abide in every human soul, and it is true that everyone can and must sooner or later find them for himself.

www.ingramcontent.com/pod-product-compliance
Lightning Source LLC
Chambersburg PA
CBHW010717080426
42450CB00035B/3447